FIFTEEN MINUTE MEALS

KT-211-122

FIFTEEN MINUTE MEALS

by Emalee Chapman

book design and illustration
by Alice Harth

101 Productions
San Francisco

Third Printing   October, 1982

Copyright © 1981 Emalee Chapman
Drawings copyright © 1981 Alice Harth
Back page quote courtesy *House & Garden.*
Copyright © 1981 by
The Condé Nast Publications Inc.

All rights reserved. No part of this book may be
reproduced in any form without the permission of
101 Productions.

Printed and bound in the United States of America.

Distributed to the book trade in the United States
by Charles Scribner's Sons, New York.

Published by 101 Productions
834 Mission Street
San Francisco, California 94103

Library of Congress Cataloging in Publication Data

Chapman, Emalee.
  Fifteen-minute meals.

  1. Cookery.   I. Harth, Alice.   II. Title.
TX652.C483   641.5'55   81-9567
ISBN 0-89286-192-4   AACR2

CONTENTS

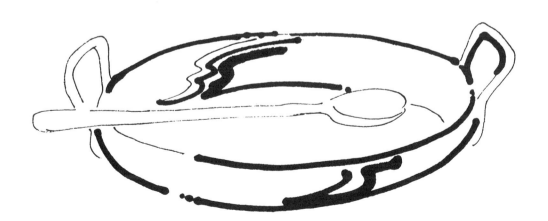

FIFTEEN MINUTES is all you need… you can cook a delicious meal in that time. My book is for busy people who are involved with work, children, projects; people who have full working days, rushed schedules and meals.

If you are looking for a good meal in a hurry, my recipes will help you to plan, to organize, and to cook quickly and effortlessly with fresh foods, saving your time, energy, money, and fuel. If you don't want to go out again at the end of the day, if you want to eat delicious food with a minimum of preparation and cooking, my recipes are for you. You will be able to eat in less time than it takes to thaw a frozen dinner or call for a pizza or make a reservation in a restaurant, and you won't be faced with the expense and hazards of eating out.

My emphasis is on how to eat well with the fresh foods nature offers, as busy people need a healthy diet for energy and stamina (and body care). The most inexperienced can prepare my recipes in a tiny kitchen with a bare-basic collection of pots, pans, and tools. I have considered the facts of our times: Food and fuel are expensive; there is less space for storage, cooking, and eating in small apartments; and

where are the helping hands in the kitchen to slice, chop, and wash?

This is a simple approach to cooking and entertaining, too. You will be able to have fast and delicious meals with ease and imagination, and you will want to use my recipes again and again for yourself, family, and friends in a variety of combinations. All of the following recipes can be easily increased to serve 3–4; when the amounts of ingredients are increased, cooking times will be slightly longer.

With the collection of recipes in this book come many pleasant memories: cooking lessons in my kitchen and lunches in my garden on Telegraph Hill with my students; lessons in France and Italy with chefs, learning the art and economy and discipline of preparing food; delightful meals with my children while living in Italy and France; Easter in Rome with special breads; summers in Rimini, on Elba; a spring picnic on the way to Venice in a field of wheat and red poppies. We spent many hours fascinated with the open food markets, the children buying local bread and cheese for meals and fresh produce to cook in our small kitchens in Florence and Paris.

I hope you will use and enjoy my collection of recipes.

METHODS: KEEP IT SIMPLE

My approach is simple: cooking fast and delicious meals using fresh foods, with shortcuts that save time and money. In this book I have adapted and impro-vised on classic European techniques; I have eliminated all unnecessary steps in preparation and cooking whenever possible.

● Save precious time by preheating the oven at the beginning of the recipe; if the recipe calls for boiling water, put it on to boil at the beginning of your preparations and use the waiting time to prepare vegetables and meats, or to make a sauce or a dessert.

● Wash all fruits and vegetables care-fully under tap water before using. Wash, but do not peel, as the nutrients are in the skin. If you don't like the skins in the sauce, strain after cooking; the minerals and vitamins will remain.

● Slice or coarsely chop vegetables and fruits before cooking; you will need less water and they will cook more quickly—and remain crisp and crunchy.

● My sauces are thickened by very fast boiling over high heat rather than with the addition of flour or other thickening agents. By using high heat and boiling, a sauce will reduce in quantity and thicken, becoming more

concentrated and flavorful. Less seasoning is needed in a reduced sauce, so add seasoning at the end of cooking, after tasting.

• Foods do not need to be excessively salted. When you are using salty ingredients such as cheese and ham, less salt is needed. Salt is easy to add but impossible to remove, and the less you use, the better for your health. I use a minimum amount of salt; I encourage the use of herbs because they enhance food with a subtle flavor.

• With meals and entertaining more relaxed today, and less space in most kitchens for storage, I have suggested basics for cooking and serving: one type of wine glass, the all-purpose tulip; the best knives, easy to keep sharp; a blender or a food processor; the heaviest pots and pans, to retain heat; one or two lids to use for all your pans.

STOCKING UP AT THE SUPERMARKET

Your raw materials should be of the best quality. It is necessary to keep some canned and frozen basics on your shelves for instant meals, but the major part of your food should be fresh, as nature's raw products have essential vitamins and minerals. Fresh food is pleasing to the eye, good to taste, and easy to cook; when food is fresh, it needs little preparation.

Shop for food once a week in markets with daily deliveries of fresh fruits and vegetables, eggs, and bread; fresh fruits and vegetables in season are cheaper than processed. Shop in markets where the produce is displayed in bulk, so you can choose each green bean, pea pod, tomato, or head of lettuce to be certain they are ripe, fresh, and unbruised.

If you don't want to waste your precious time standing in lines, shop on a weekday, at night, or early in the morning, when the stores are not so crowded. Buy nonperishable groceries in quantity when the price is low, but don't overbuy. Food and fuel are expensive, so save your dollars and time by buying only what you need: the small can of corn, or the half-dozen eggs; if you make a list, you will know.

Vegetables and fruits should not be washed until ready to use; just refrigerate them in the vegetable compartment or shelf. Grains and flours should be stored in closed containers; oils stay fresher in a dark, cool cupboard.

Your pleasure in food shopping and cooking will increase if you become more curious and flexible about trying ethnic variations in foods. Explore the markets in your area for breads in different shapes and textures; look for seasonal produce and fresh herbs, spring lamb, and crab in season. Surprise yourself with imaginative, easy meals.

WHAT TO KEEP IN CUPBOARD, REFRIGERATOR, AND FREEZER

Thinking of food before you go to work in the morning is difficult to manage because time is so short. Often you get home late; by the time you have read the mail and kicked off your shoes, the telephone has rung four times, and it is nearly eight o'clock. This means scanning the refrigerator shelves to look for what can be made quickly. So your meals will depend on a well-stocked cupboard and food bought once a week; it is important that you keep the basic necessities on your shelves and in the refrigerator and freezer.

Keep the essentials on hand and you will always have a fast and satisfying meal.

BASIC FOODS TO KEEP
ON THE CUPBOARD SHELVES

Anchovies, canned Delicious in mayonnaise, to flavor sauces, with veal.

Black olives, canned

Clam juice, bottled For poaching fish, for sauces and soups.

Crab, tuna, and salmon, canned

Beans, canned White *cannellini,* and red kidney beans for salads.

Bouillon cubes Chicken and beef; choose a brand without salt and additives.

Chocolate, 2–3-ounce bars Italian, French, or Swiss.

Cocoa, Dutch To make brownies, instant desserts.

Cornmeal, yellow Packaged; for corn muffins, quick meals.

Flour A small package, for cooking and baking.

Herbs Buy fresh when available; buy dried in small quantities.*

Jams and jellies Apricot jam, plum jam, and currant jelly for cooking meats and fruits.

Oil Safflower is the lightest, least fattening.

Olive oil French or Italian.

Pasta, dry, in packages, imported from Italy Spaghetti, long and thin, and all other shapes; buy the smallest sizes, riso and stelline, for quick meals.

Peppercorns Whole black, green, and white (not as strong), for cooking and for grinding fresh in a peppermill.

Rice For risottos, soups, salads; the plump Italian Arborio variety is best, and easiest to cook.

Sea salt Gives a crunchy texture to salads; has best flavor.

Semolina Fine hard-wheat flour; can be found in 16-ounce packages and in bulk in Italian markets; it is cheap, and easy to prepare for an instant meal.

Sugar, brown, granulated, and powdered For desserts, fruits.

Vinegar, red wine and white wine

*Bottled herbs and condiments are high-cost items on supermarket shelves. Bottled herbs on the market shelf are not always fresh, as they lose their flavor after a few months. Buy fresh herbs when you see them and dry a small bunch by your stove. They cost less and have more strength and flavor than the bottled. Crush a bit in your fingers when you want to add a subtle taste to a sauce. Use less of dried herbs in your cooking, as their flavor is stronger than fresh. Used in moderation, herbs will enhance your cooking. Dried green celery leaves will add flavor to soups and salads.

BASIC FOODS TO KEEP IN THE REFRIGERATOR

Beans, green

Bread

Butter, unsalted

Cheese One pound Parmesan, freshly grated

Cream Heavy or whipping, without additives.

Eggs Buy only what you need.

Fruit

Lemons

Lettuce

Mustard, Dijon

Paprika Hungarian is sweetest; buy a small amount.

Parsley Store unwashed in vegetable compartment, but not in plastic.

Potatoes, small new

Zucchini

BASIC FOODS TO KEEP IN THE FREEZER

Bread Keeps well.

Broth, any leftover

Butter, unsalted

Frozen packages of:

　*Beans, green**

　*Peas**

　*Spinach**

　Raspberries For instant jams, sauces, desserts

　Strawberries For instant jams, sauces, desserts

*Buy plain vegetables, frozen without sugar or sauces.

KITCHEN EQUIPMENT

The kitchens of some of the best cooks I know are small. The size of the kitchen isn't important, but the space should be well planned, the equipment and tools well organized. A tiny kitchen can be made efficient with proper tools well placed with thought and care; pots, pans, and tools can be hung to save space.

Learning what equipment should be used and why is all important. This will help you to collect the essentials, to eliminate and substitute for what you don't need, and to know how to buy what you need. There are certain items in my kitchen that I could not do without: my blender, sauté pans, knives, mixing bowls of all sizes, and my wooden chopping block.

The proper tools must be thoughtfully chosen and maintained. The best equipment is not necessarily the most expensive, but you must know what to look for when you buy. Price does not always reflect quality: There are excellent measuring cups, spoons, sieves, enameled pans and muffin tins in dime stores.

You should start by buying only the absolute essentials: knives of the best quality that will take sharp edges, heavy pans that retain heat without burning. Well-made equipment can last a lifetime. You will add to your basics as you develop the need. Knowing your tools, which pot or pan or knife to use, will help to improve your skill in the kitchen and to achieve quickly and with a minimum of effort simple, delicious meals.

I have made my suggested list of kitchen equipment as practical and basic as possible, considering economy of space and money, and your need for good, fast meals; no large pots, ring molds, or exotic tins for bombes and pâtés here.

CUTLERY BASICS:
THE MOST ESSENTIAL

You will be impatient with a dull knife. High-carbon stainless steel takes a good sharp edge and will resist rust, acid, and salt; good knives are well constructed and made of the best metals. They will last a lifetime with care. The heavy hardwood handle should feel balanced in your hand, easy to use and to control.

Boning knife Has a thin, flexible blade 4–8 inches long with a fine-pointed razor-sharp tip; for chicken, fish, meat.

Chef's knife For chopping vegetables, slicing carrots, cabbage. Has a 10–12-inch blade.

Paring knife A small chef's knife with a rigid triangular blade 3–4 inches long. For preparing vegetables and fruit.

Serrated bread knife Has a blunt tip and a 10–12-inch blade.

Serrated knife Needs no sharpening; for cutting fruit with tough skins, such as oranges, tomatoes, artichokes.

Slicing knife With a 10-inch blade for slicing long, thin slices of meat, and for carving poultry.

Rinse your knives after using, wipe them immediately, and return them to drawer or rack. Never leave your knives in the sink, and never, never soak them in water. I keep my knives in a drawer with separate compartments for each knife; I put a used wine-bottle cork on each sharp point (learned from the French) to protect the tip. I take my knives to a professional once a year to have them sharpened. You may want to use a sharpening steel to keep your blades sharp, but do not use an electric sharpener, as it wears the blade.

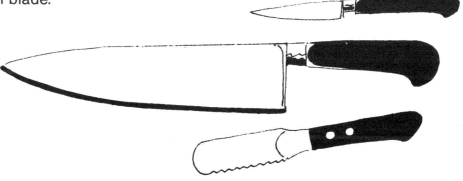

POTS, PANS, AND OVEN DISHES: THE MOST VERSATILE

Individual (4–7-ounce) custard cups or bowls, 4 Stoneware or porcelain with glazed interiors, for baking purées (will not pick up and transfer flavors), eggs, puddings, and custards, and for sauces to take to the table.

Mixing bowls, 5 Heavyweight ceramic or earthenware with glazed interiors and flat bases so they will not tip with vigorous beating. Graduated sizes ranging in capacity from 16 ounces to 3 quarts—2 small, 2 medium, 1 large—for beating eggs, mixing ingredients, for desserts, vegetables, salads, and to take to the table. A 1-1/2-quart glazed ceramic pudding bowl will not crack when put into boiling water to melt chocolate, or make custard sauces and scrambled eggs; the flat bottom is good for beating egg whites.

Oven dishes, 2 Oval shaped; 1 medium sized, 14 inches long; 1 small, 9 inches long, good for 2 portions. They should be shallow fireproof porcelain, earthenware, or enameled cast iron, to be used in the oven to bake fowl, fish, meat, vegetables, or fruit, and to go to the table for serving. These are best for dishes with acidic sauces with tomatoes or wine, since the interaction of metal with foods will often discolor a sauce or change the flavor.

Oven sheet Heavy-duty carbon-steel sheet; a must for grilling and baking, making toast, canapés. Fourteen inches diameter round.

Roasting dish Oval or square, 16 inches long, medium sized; it should be copper, iron, or metal to take high heat for roasting meat or fowl.

Saucepans, 2 One 2-quart and one 4–5-quart; deep pans of enameled iron or tin-lined copper with a heat-resistant handle (for acidic fruits and vegetables). Use the small pan for boiling liquids, vegetables, fruit, and quickly reduced sauces; the straight sides contain heat, allowing liquids to cook at a gentle simmer or a fast boil. Use the large saucepan for boiling broth, pasta, potatoes.

Sauté pans, 2 One small, 6–7 inches in diameter (you can make a soufflé in this pan); 1 medium sized, 8 inches in diameter, for 2 people. A heavy, shallow, straight-sided pan in which small cuts of meat, poultry, and vegetables can be cooked in butter or oil; the wide, flat bottoms slide easily across a burner, and the straight 3-inch-high sides prevent foods from jumping out as you stir; food being sautéed should not be crowded. A skillet can be used if you don't have a sauté pan. Sauté pans or skillets should be cast iron, copper with a tin lining, carbon steel, or heavy-gauge aluminum. The metal must be able to absorb direct heat evenly (enamel will not take high heat).

Lids You need only one large lid for your pans, as a large lid will cover both large and small pans. It will work best if flat, with a handle.

Learn to care for your pans and oven dishes. If food burns or sticks, cover the bottom with baking soda and fill the pan with hot water to soak. After using pots and pans, rinse with hot water immediately; they will be ready to use again. I learned to clean my copper from the smart, thrifty French (in cooking school): Don't discard the lemon skin after squeezing lemon juice; saturate the inside with rock salt to rub over and polish your copper pots and pans.

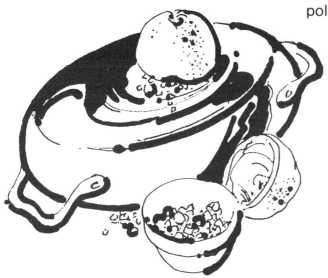

TOOLS:
SUGGESTED BARE NECESSITIES

Basic, bare-minimum tools for cooking for 2–4 people:

Blender or food processor Keep where it is always available for instant use.

Chopping board Keep conveniently at hand.

Colander For draining lettuce, large vegetables, pasta.

Corkscrew For removing corks from bottles.

Fork, wooden handle For turning meat in pan.

Grater, upright For cheese and vegetables (unless you have a food processor).

Manual can opener Dependable.

Measuring cups A basic set of stainless steel cups for dry measuring: a Pyrex cup holding 2–4 cups for liquids.

Measuring spoons Each one clearly labeled.

Pepper mill For freshly ground pepper.

Sieve with fine mesh For draining and straining.

Spatulas Rubber, for removing food from bowls, blender; metal, for removing hot foods from oven sheets and pans, and for spreading butter.

Whisk or egg beater For egg whites, yolks, whipped cream, stirring lumps out of sauces.

Wooden spoons, 4 For stirring sauces and soups.

Think about your work areas: Put your chopping block where you will cut and slice vegetables, meat, bread. Counter space should be reserved for food preparation and mixing, a place where you can lay out your supplies. Equipment should be kept near the area where it will be used: Store pots and pans and the tools most often used for cooking—spatulas, wooden spoons, whisks—near the stove to be at hand when you need them.

The blender takes over time-consuming blending, puréeing, and chopping chores; the food processor performs magic with its ability to grate, slice, and shred. Both machines make it possible to use all scraps and leftovers for soups, sauces. Since you do not have hours to spend on labor and preparations, you should have at least one of these multipurpose tools.

Eggs provide an infinite variety of dishes. They can be cooked with vegetables, made into omelets and fritters and baked as custards, used in sauces, and cooked in their shells. With an egg or two you can make an appetizer, a light first course or a dazzling soufflé to serve as a complete meal. One egg can be a meal in itself to take to bed on a tray after a long day.

All domestic birds' eggs can be eaten, including those of quail. The tiny eggs of quail are very decorative, with shells of exquisite pale-blue or brown speckles, and they have a lovely flavor. Simmered gently in their shells, quail eggs can be served as an appetizer with thinly sliced bread, butter, and paprika.

Here are a few basic rules for eggs: Buy your eggs as fresh as possible; refrigerate in their cardboard cartons to prevent absorbing odors from other foods (unless it is a truffle). Don't overcook your eggs. Eggs don't like high heat; they become hard and indigestible (a soufflé is the exception to this rule). Don't overbeat egg whites or they will be dry and difficult to mix with other ingredients, and they will lose their buoyancy. Don't underbeat yolks; they should be creamy and light colored, with increased volume.

SMOKED SALMON WITH SCRAMBLED EGGS

The Café Flore on the left bank has the best scrambled eggs in Paris, although few people know about them; most of the mix of people that go there—writers, fashion freaks, artists, film-makers—have drinks or coffee. This dish is for that night when you feel like taking something light to bed to eat on a tray.

4 eggs
4 tablespoons warm water
6 thin slices smoked salmon, cut into
  slivers
Freshly ground black pepper

1. Lightly beat eggs in a bowl with a whisk or egg beater, adding water.
2. Put some water in a saucepan; bring to boiling and put bowl with eggs over water; cooked like this they will be creamier.
3. Lower heat; stir eggs constantly, as they will cook quickly; stir in slivers of smoked salmon and pepper to taste. Serves 2.

BAKED CHEESE OMELET

This is a very creamy omelet.

Preheat oven to 450°F
1 tablespoon unsalted butter
2 eggs
1 cup cottage cheese
1/2 cup grated Gruyère or cheddar
  cheese

1. Butter a medium-sized oven dish.
2. Beat eggs lightly, adding cottage cheese, or blend together briefly in a blender.
3. Pour egg mixture into oven dish; sprinkle with grated cheese.
4. Bake 10 minutes in *preheated* oven. Serves 2.

ASPARAGUS WITH EGGS SUNNY-SIDE-UP

In Milano this dish is called "Sunny-Side-Up." I have had these delicious eggs many times in a small restaurant, located in Milan's Galleria, where there are simple, good food and a very friendly ambiance.

Preheat oven to 400°F
2 tablespoons unsalted butter
8 asparagus tips, canned, fresh or
  frozen (cut fresh tips off at 3 inches)
4 slices prosciutto
4 eggs
1/2 cup grated Parmesan cheese
Freshly ground black pepper

1. Heat butter in a sauté pan or skillet; add asparagus tips and cook in butter for 2 minutes.
2. Place slices of prosciutto on bottom of a medium-sized oven dish, break eggs into dish over ham, and sprinkle 1/4 cup cheese over eggs. Pour asparagus and all butter and juices from pan over eggs; sprinkle remaining grated cheese over all.
3. Place in *preheated* oven about 5 minutes, depending on how well cooked you like your eggs. Season to taste with pepper.
Serves 2.

LETTUCE FRITTATA

A French chef taught me never to throw away even one wilted lettuce leaf. This dish is best with the outer leaves of romaine lettuce.

Preheat broiler at full broil
1 tablespoon unsalted butter
1 cup coarsely chopped romaine lettuce
   leaves
2 eggs
Sea salt
Freshly ground black pepper
1/4 cup grated Gruyère cheese

1. Heat butter in a sauté pan or skillet; add lettuce and cook, stirring, for 2 minutes.
2. Beat eggs in a small bowl; add seasoning to taste and pour over lettuce.
3. Let cook gently over medium heat until set on bottom, about 2 minutes.
4. Sprinkle grated cheese over top. Put pan under *preheated* broiler until cheese melts and top puffs, about 1 minute. Take pan to table to serve hot.
Serves 2.

SOUFFLE FOR TWO

A soufflé cooks more quickly in a wide, shallow pan than in a deep dish; use your medium-sized sauté pan or skillet for this soufflé.

Preheat oven to 475°F
4 eggs, at room temperature
3 ounces cream cheese
2 thin slices prosciutto
1/2 cup grated Monterey Jack cheese
Freshly ground black pepper

1. Separate eggs. Put egg yolks in a blender with cream cheese and prosciutto; purée. Stir in cheese and season to taste with pepper.
2. With an egg beater or whisk, whip whites to soft, not dry, peaks.
3. Fold yolk mixture quickly and lightly into whites; spoon into a sauté pan or skillet and place in *preheated* hot oven. The soufflé will take 10-12 minutes to cook. The outside of the finished soufflé should be brown and crusty and the inside (center) still creamy and liquid, to be used as a sauce.
Serves 2.

APPETIZERS

Appealing appetizers can be made with eggs, cheese, vegetables, ham, and fish. Choose your ingredients with care and keep appetizers light: Don't spoil appetites for the meal to come.

CORN CRISPS

A tasty appetizer with a drink.

Preheat oven to 450°F
1 cup yellow cornmeal
2 cups boiling water
3 tablespoons unsalted butter
1/8 teaspoon cayenne
1 egg, well beaten
1/2 cup poppy seeds

1. Measure cornmeal into a bowl and pour boiling water over.
2. Add butter and cayenne to bowl and let sit for 2 minutes until cornmeal thickens.
3. Stir in well-beaten egg; with a teaspoon drop small rounds (the size of a half-dollar) onto a baking sheet and sprinkle poppy seeds over each one.
4. Bake in *preheated* oven until brown on edges, about 8–10 minutes.
Makes 30 crisps.

The smaller you make the crisps, the faster they will bake. If you want to make just a few crisps, place extra batter in refrigerator; it will keep 2–3 days.

Variation   Instead of poppy seeds, stir 1/2 cup grated Parmesan cheese into batter.

CHEESE APPETIZER

Preheat broiler at full broil
4 slices thin white bread
1 cup mayonnaise
1/4 cup grated Parmesan cheese
4 parsley sprigs (no stems)

1. Remove crusts of bread with a bread knife; cut bread into small squares, or rounds with a biscuit cutter.
2. Place squares on an oven sheet and toast one side under broiler.
3. Blend mayonnaise, cheese, and parsley in a blender. Pile 1–2 teaspoons of mixture in a high mound on untoasted side of each toast square.
4. Place under *preheated* broiler until mixture puffs and browns, about 1 minute.
Makes 16 canapés.

Serve hot, on a napkin-covered plate.

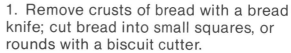

DROP BISCUITS

Preheat oven to 450°F
1 cup flour
1 teaspoon baking powder
3 tablespoons soft butter
About 1/4–1/2 cup milk

1. Measure flour and baking powder into a bowl.
2. Add butter to bowl and rub butter into flour with your fingers or a fork.
3. Add milk to make a thick batter, stirring only until dough sticks together.
4. Drop by teaspoonfuls on an ungreased baking sheet. Bake 7–8 minutes in *preheated* oven.
Makes 12 biscuits.

Variation For a hot appetizer: Roll each piece of dough in soft butter, then in grated Parmesan cheese and paprika; bake in a hot oven 7–8 minutes, until brown.

CHEESE BISCUITS

Easy to make; wonderful to eat. I first had these in Paris with an apéritif.

Preheat oven to 400°F
1/4 pound (1/2 cup) soft unsalted
   butter
1 cup grated sharp cheddar cheese
1 cup flour
1/8 teaspoon cayenne
1/8 teaspoon paprika

1. Mix butter and cheese together in a small bowl with a fork or your fingers or in a food processor; add flour and seasonings.
2. Form into a ball with your hands; press dough flat on a board, patting thin.
3. Cut into rounds with a biscuit cutter or the rim of a glass.
4. Bake in *preheated* oven 7–8 minutes.
Makes 24 biscuits.

Serve hot or cold; nice with soups and salads, too. Make as many as you wish; refrigerate extra dough.

MANGO AND PROSCIUTTO

Fresh fruit with the salty taste of prosciutto makes an appetizing bite served on a toothpick.

1 mango, peeled and sliced thin
6 slices prosciutto, fat removed
Freshly ground black pepper
1 lemon, cut into quarters

1. Wrap each slice of mango with a thin piece of prosciutto.
2. Arrange on a plate, grind black pepper over, and garnish with lemon quarters.
Makes 6–12 appetizers, depending upon size.

CORN PANCAKES

These delicious small pancakes make an easy appetizer to start your meal; or try them with a slice of ham and a green salad.

One 8–9-ounce can whole-kernel corn
  (1 cup)
1 egg
1/4 cup flour
1/2 teaspoon baking powder
1/4 teaspoon cayenne
1/4 teaspoon paprika
1 tablespoon unsalted butter

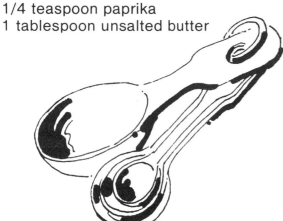

1. Place all ingredients, except butter, in a blender. Blend briefly; mixture should be coarse, with texture.
2. Heat 1 teaspoon butter in a sauté pan or skillet; when hot (a drop of water shaken into pan will jump) drop in tablespoonfuls of batter, widely spaced.
3. Lower heat; cakes should cook slowly to a golden brown.
4. When crisp on bottoms, cakes will turn easily; when golden on both sides, remove to a warm dish. Add 1 teaspoon butter to pan and repeat process; serve hot.
Makes 12 pancakes.

LIGHT DISHES

Any one of these dishes, with a minimum of effort, can be a light meal or a pleasant prelude; serve with the greenest of salads.

SEMOLINA

Semolina is a fine, light-yellow meal, the hard-wheat flour used to make pasta in Italy; it can be found in Italian markets in 7- or 16-ounce packages, or it can be bought in bulk. I always keep a pound on the cupboard shelf, as it makes a fast, satisfying meal.

Preheat broiler at full broil
1 cup milk
1 cup water
5 tablespoons semolina
2 tablespoons unsalted butter
1/2 cup grated Parmesan cheese
1 teaspoon Dijon mustard

1. Combine milk and water in a medium-sized saucepan and bring to a boil over high heat.
2. Lower heat to a simmer after liquid has come to a boil. Stir semolina into pan 1 tablespoonful at a time so it doesn't lump. It will bubble slowly and thicken in about 4 minutes.
3. Remove pan from heat; add butter, 1/4 cup cheese, and mustard, mixing well.
4. Pour semolina into a buttered flat oven dish, smoothing evenly with a tablespoon.
5. Sprinkle 1/4 cup cheese over top and place under *preheated* broiler to brown for 1 minute. Take dish to the table to serve hot.
Serves 2.

GIANT PUFF

Try making this giant popover; it is crisp and puffy, almost a soufflé. Have it with a bowl of soup or a salad.

Preheat oven to 475–500°F (this is very important; let oven heat to full temperature)
Have ready 1 heavy 9–10-inch sauté pan or skillet
3 tablespoons unsalted butter
2 eggs
1/2 cup flour
1/2 cup milk
1/4 cup grated Gruyère cheese

1. Melt butter in a sauté pan or skillet in oven; use same pan to bake puff.
2. Blend eggs, flour, and milk in a blender, pouring in melted butter.
3. Pour into pan and sprinkle grated cheese over; place in *preheated hot* oven. Bake 10–12 minutes. This puff should be dark brown and crusty outside, soft inside.
Serves 2.

SPINACH CREPES

Bright green pancakes with a tasty filling; this is all you need for a light supper. You can use a sauté pan or skillet (a crêpe pan is shallow and made of carbon steel with flaring sides to allow crêpes to slide out of pan; it has a diameter of seven inches).

Preheat oven to 375°F
1/2 cup small spinach leaves (no stems)
1 egg
3 tablespoons unsalted butter, melted
1/2 cup flour
3/4 cup milk
6 mushrooms
1/2 cup sour cream
1 thin slice boiled ham
1/4 teaspoon paprika
1/4 cup grated Gruyère cheese

1. Make crêpe batter first, as it should sit a few minutes. Wash spinach leaves and put into a blender. Add egg, butter, flour, and milk; blend well for 1 minute; pour into a bowl.

2. Wash mushrooms carefully and purée in blender with sour cream, ham, and paprika.

3. Heat a small sauté pan or skillet over medium heat until a drop of water jumps in pan (no need to butter pan).

4. Put 1 tablespoon batter into hot pan and roll pan to spread batter evenly.

Reduce heat; crêpe will cook in 1/2 minute; crêpes should be thin and so don't need to be turned. Thin batter with 1–2 tablespoons water as you make crêpes because batter will thicken as it stands; crêpes should be *very* thin.

5. Place crêpes in an oven dish as you make them; spread filling over each one and fold. Sprinkle grated cheese over crêpes; put dish in *preheated* oven 2–3 minutes.

Makes 12 crêpes.

VEGETABLES are best—tender and sweet—when young and small. Vegetables should be carefully selected, one by one, as if picking a bouquet of flowers. Nothing can make old, soft, wilted vegetables taste fresh. Buy your vegetables at the peak of their season from a market that has daily deliveries from the produce market. Fresh vegetables not only taste better, but they are an economy, as they will last longer in your refrigerator, and you will not have to market as often.

Doctors and nutritionists increasingly emphasize the value of fresh raw vegetables and herbs in a basic daily diet for those who want to protect the body and stay well. Eat the skins of vegetables, since the skin contains many nutrients.

By chopping or slicing vegetables, you will shorten the cooking time, your vegetables will be tender and crisp, and you will avoid overcooking. Also, you won't need as much water in the pan, as the natural juices will slip out in cooking, and this is where the vitamins are. Instead of a high-calorie sauce, use the pan liquid as a sauce for your vegetables.

The possibilities of vegetable combinations are endless. Sometimes after a long working day, light vegetable dishes may seem more appealing for dinner than complicated, heavier dishes.

QUICKLY COOKED ARTICHOKES

2 artichokes
1/4 cup olive oil
1 garlic clove, peeled
1/2 cup water
Sea salt
Freshly ground black pepper

1. With a chef's knife cut off artichoke stems at base and cut artichokes into quarters; remove inner whiskers and pull off tough outer leaves.
2. Warm oil in a sauté pan or skillet, add whole garlic clove, and cook 1 minute.
3. Put quartered artichokes and stems in pan and cook 1 minute in hot oil, turning artichokes in oil; remove garlic with a spoon.
4. Pour water into pan, bring to boil, and cook 5 minutes; turn artichokes to cook on other side, cover pan, and cook 5 minutes.
5. Season to taste, remove from pan, and serve at room temperature.
Serves 2.

Don't serve artichokes with wine, because artichokes and wine don't mix.

ASPARAGUS PUREE

10–12 green asparagus
1 cup water
1 tablespoon unsalted butter
1/4 cup heavy cream
1/4 cup grated Parmesan cheese
Freshly ground black pepper

1. With a chef's knife cut tips from asparagus so you have 3-inch lengths.
2. Bring water to boil in a sauté pan or skillet, add tips, and boil slowly 4–5 minutes.
3. Drain into a sieve; put into a blender and purée, adding butter and cream.
4. Empty into a bowl and stir in cheese and pepper to taste.
Serves 2.

Very colorful served with carrot purée.

Variation Do not purée asparagus; serve whole with butter, cheese, and pepper to taste.

Variation To make cream of asparagus soup, pour cooked asparagus and cooking liquid into a blender to purée; add cream, butter, cheese, and pepper.

BROCCOLI

Try cooking your broccoli as
the Romans do:

3 stalks broccoli
1/4 cup safflower oil
1 garlic clove, peeled and cut in half
1 cup white wine
Sea salt
Freshly ground black pepper

1. Wash broccoli and cut off tough
stems, leaving the green leaves; chop
broccoli coarsely with a chef's knife.
2. Heat oil in a sauté pan or skillet; add
garlic clove halves and cook until golden;
remove garlic with a spoon.
3. Add broccoli, mixing with oil until
pieces glisten.
4. Pour in wine and simmer over medium
heat for 6 minutes, until tender; season
to taste.
5. Pour liquid from pan over broccoli
and serve.
Serves 2.

WHITE BEANS WITH TOMATOES

In a Florentine restaurant there is always
a dish of these pink-white beans glistening in oil.

One 16-ounce can white kidney beans
   (cannellini)
2 tablespoons olive oil
4 fresh sage leaves, or 1 teaspoon
   dried sage
2 unpeeled ripe tomatoes
Sea salt
Freshly ground black pepper
1 tablespoon wine vinegar

1. Drain beans in a sieve.
2. Heat oil in a saucepan; add sage and
cook in hot oil 1 minute.
3. Cut tomatoes into pan and stir in
beans; cover and simmer over medium
heat 8–9 minutes.
4. Season to taste; add vinegar and stir
all together well.
Serves 2.

GREEN BEANS

2 cups water
1/2 pound green beans
1 lemon
2 tablespoons olive oil
4 parsley sprigs, chopped (no stems)
Sea salt
Freshly ground black pepper

1. Pour water into sauté pan or skillet and place over medium heat.
2. Snap ends to tear off any strings and break beans in half into water in pan.
3. Cook uncovered 4–5 minutes; beans should be crisp.
4. Drain beans in a sieve and place in a bowl.
5. Squeeze lemon juice into bowl over beans; add oil, parsley, and seasoning to taste.
Serves 2.

RED CABBAGE AND APPLES

2 tablespoons unsalted butter
2 unpeeled yellow apples
2 cups chopped red cabbage
1/4 cup red wine
3 tablespoons red currant jelly

1. Melt butter over low heat in a sauté pan or skillet; slice apples into pan and add cabbage, stirring. Cook 5 minutes over medium heat.
2. Stir in wine and jelly. Cover pan and cook 6–7 minutes.
Serves 2.

CARROT PUREE

1 tablespoon unsalted butter
6 small unpeeled carrots
3 tablespoons Marsala wine
4 parsley sprigs (no stems)
4 tablespoons sour cream or plain
   yogurt
Freshly ground black pepper

1. Melt butter in a sauté pan or skillet.
2. Wash carrots and slice into pan; stir with butter.
3. Add Marsala to pan, cover, and cook 5 minutes over low heat.
4. Put carrots into blender with parsley and sour cream; purée.
5. Place in a bowl and season with pepper to taste.
Serves 2.

CAULIFLOWER

2 cups water
1 small cauliflower
4 tablespoons safflower oil
2 tablespoons wine vinegar
Sea salt
Freshly ground black pepper
6 parsley sprigs (no stems)

1. Bring water to boiling in a saucepan.
2. Wash cauliflower and cut into quarters, leaving green leaves.
3. Add cauliflower quarters to boiling water, cover pan, lower heat, and simmer 8 minutes.
3. Mix oil and vinegar in a bowl to make dressing; season to taste.
4. Drain cauliflower in a colander and place in bowl with dressing.
5. Chop parsley very fine with a chef's knife and sprinkle over cauliflower; serve at room temperature.
Serves 2.

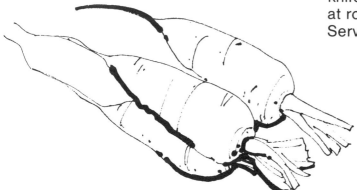

CELERY ROOT

I had this dish in a crowded, noisy, small bar-restaurant across the street from Dior in Paris where there were exotic models, attractive people speaking rapidly in many languages, thick smoke from French tobacco, and the best snacks in Paris.

2 cups water
1 small celery root
1 lemon
1 small unpeeled ripe tomato
1/2 cup heavy cream
1 teaspoon Dijon mustard
Sea salt
Paprika

1. Heat water in a saucepan.
2. With a sharp knife peel outside knobby skin off celery root.
3. Slice celery root into a pan and squeeze juice of lemon over slices; when water boils, reduce heat and simmer 8 minutes.
4. Drain in a colander, pour into a bowl, and mix with this sauce:
5. Cut tomato into a blender, add cream and mustard, and purée. Pour into a bowl and season to taste.
Serves 2.

Variation After simmering, purée drained celery root in a blender with 1/2 cup heavy cream, 1 teaspoon butter, and salt and paprika to taste.

CAULIFLOWER PUREE

1 cup cooked cauliflower
2 tablespoons sour cream or plain
  yogurt
6 parsley sprigs (no stems)
Paprika

1. Put cooked cauliflower into a blender with sour cream and parsley and blend.
2. Pour into a bowl and season with paprika to taste.
Serves 2.

FENNEL

7–8 fennel stalks (celery can be used
   in place of fennel)
2 tablespoons unsalted butter
1 cup water or broth
Sea salt
Freshly ground white pepper

1. Chop fennel coarsely with a chef's
knife while heating butter in a sauté
pan or skillet.
2. Put fennel into pan with butter and
stir over medium-low heat for 2 minutes,
coating fennel well with butter.
3. Add water to pan and bring to a
boil;cook rapidly 4–5 minutes to reduce
and thicken liquid, making a sauce.
Watch pan while cooking; if too much
water evaporates, add a little more.
4. Season fennel to taste and serve.
Serves 2.

MUSHROOMS

Mushrooms have a strong, fresh flavor and are low in calories.

8–10 unpeeled mushrooms
1 tablespoon unsalted butter
1 cup sour cream
4 parsley sprigs, chopped (no stems)
Sea salt
Freshly ground black pepper

1. Wash mushrooms carefully under cold water; don't soak.
2. Melt butter in a sauté pan or skillet; slice mushrooms into pan and cook, stirring, 3 minutes.
3. Stir in sour cream and parsley and cook for 1 minute.
4. Season to taste and serve.
Serves 2.

Very good with a broiled veal chop.

SLICED MUSHROOMS

Good with ground veal patties.

8 unpeeled mushrooms
2 tablespoons unsalted butter
1/4 cup white wine
Paprika
1 lemon, cut in half

1. Wash mushrooms carefully and cut into thin slices.
2. Melt butter in a sauté pan or skillet, add mushrooms, and cook slowly over medium heat 2 minutes.
3. Pour in wine, cook for 3 minutes, and season to taste with paprika.
3. Garnish with lemon halves and serve.
Serves 2.

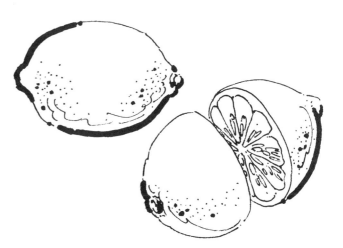

NUTRITIOUS NEW RED POTATOES

Small new red potatoes are the most nutritious member of the potato family; they have a firm texture and good flavor. Leave the skin on, for the vitamins. Starchy vegetables, such as potatoes, should never be served chilled, for they lose their flavor and become indigestible. Potato salad is best served at room temperature.

3 cups water
8–10 unpeeled small new red potatoes
1/4 cup safflower oil
1/4 cup dry white wine
4 parsley sprigs, chopped (no stems)
Sea salt
Freshly ground black pepper

1. Pour water into a sauté pan or skillet and place over high heat; slice potatoes into water and bring to a boil.
2. Lower heat and simmer potatoes 7–8 minutes, or until tender.
3. Drain potatoes in a colander; put into a bowl and toss while warm with oil, wine, and parsley; season to taste and serve.
Serves 2.

PEAS WITH LETTUCE

Spring makes me think about the open market in Cannes: stalls heaped with mounds of vegetables; fresh fragrant herbs; bright flowers; bread baked in the shape of doves; chocolate fish, large and small, in the windows of the pastry shops—all signs of spring and Easter to come.

2 tablespoons unsalted butter
2 cups peas in the shell, or one
    10-ounce package frozen peas
2 lettuce leaves, chopped
1/2 cup chicken broth
Sea salt
Freshly ground black pepper

1. Melt butter in a sauté pan or skillet.
2. Shell peas into pan with butter.
3. Add lettuce; stir and cook for 2 minutes.
4. Pour in broth and simmer 5–6 minutes.
5. Season to taste and serve.
Serves 2.

FRESH SPINACH

1 small bunch fresh spinach
2 tablespoons safflower oil
1 lemon (grate the rind)
Sea salt
Freshly ground black pepper

1. Wash spinach leaves and chop leaves coarsely with a chef's knife; don't use stems.
2. Heat oil in a sauté pan or skillet, add spinach, and cook over medium heat 3–4 minutes.
3. Add grated rind of lemon, squeeze juice of lemon over spinach, and stir.
4. Season to taste and serve.
Serves 2.

GREEN SPINACH SAUCE

I remember with pleasure the large basket of fresh vegetables in a small restaurant on the Ile St-Louis. The waiter brought to our table a still life of crudités, a splendid assortment of raw vegetables, beautifully arranged: whole mushrooms, baby zucchini, tiny carrots, peas in crisp pods, thin asparagus, cucumber, celery stalks, fennel, endive,

and baby lettuce tucked into the corners of the basket. Another offering arrived with slices of ham, thick slices of freshly grilled toast, a sauce of crème fraîche and herbs—a lovely beginning in a romantic setting. A green sauce made with fresh spinach was put on our table to eat with the vegetables.

1 cup plain yogurt or sour cream
1 cup raw spinach leaves (no stems)
1/2 shallot, peeled
6 parsley sprigs (no stems)
Sea salt
Freshly ground black pepper

1. Put yogurt into blender with spinach, shallot, and parsley; purée.
2. Pour into a bowl and season to taste. Makes about 1 cup.

Serve with raw vegetables.

GREEN AND YELLOW SQUASH

3 unpeeled pale-green summer
  squash
3 unpeeled yellow crookneck squash
2 tablespoons unsalted butter
1/4 cup chicken broth
Sea salt
Freshly ground black pepper

1. Chop squash coarsely with a chef's knife.
2. Melt butter in a sauté pan or skillet. Stir squash into pan with butter.
3. Cook over medium heat 2 minutes, stirring; add broth.
4. Cook 5 minutes, season to taste, and serve.
Serves 2.

BROILED TOMATOES

Preheat broiler at full broil
2 unpeeled tomatoes
2 tablespoons olive oil
1 slice fresh bread
1 garlic clove, peeled
4 parsley sprigs (no stems)
Sea salt
Freshly ground black pepper

1. Cut tomatoes in half and place in an oven dish.
2. Dribble oil over tomatoes and place under *preheated* broiler 2 minutes.
3. In a blender briefly chop bread, garlic, and parsley into a coarse mixture.
4. Cover each tomato with bread crumb mixture and season to taste.
5. Return to broiler for 1–2 minutes, until golden brown; serve hot.
Serves 2.

ZUCCHINI WITH TOMATOES

We went to Siena in early summer to see the event of the year, the Palio, wild horseracing and jousting in the Piazza del Campo. The race course and the buildings are hung with medieval flags and banners, the horses are draped, and the riders are dressed in costumes of the 14th century. We had this dish in a crowded restaurant in a side street.

2 tablespoons olive oil
3 unpeeled ripe tomatoes
6 fresh basil leaves, chopped, or
    1 teaspoon dried basil
3 unpeeled zucchini

1. Pour oil into a sauté pan or skillet; while heating over medium heat, slice tomatoes into pan.
2. Add basil and cook 3 minutes with tomatoes.
3. Slice zucchini into pan and cook 5 minutes.
Serves 2.

Cooked vegetables such as this dish are delicious served either warm or at room temperature.

GRATED ZUCCHINI

Zucchini really should be picked when no larger than your finger, with the flower still clinging to them. Zucchini has a high water content and for this reason is best cooked with very little or no water.

4 unpeeled zucchini
1 lemon
Sea salt
Freshly ground black pepper

1. Grate zucchini into a sauté pan or skillet (or shred in a food processor and place in pan).
2. Place pan over high heat and stir; as zucchini starts to cook you will see water escaping.
3. Lower heat and stir constantly as zucchini cooks, 2–3 minutes.
4. Squeeze juice of lemon over zucchini, stir, and season to taste.
Serves 2.

Variation In place of lemon juice, stir 1/4 cup grated Parmesan cheese into zucchini and season to taste.

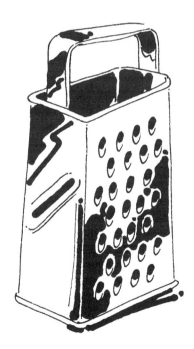

SOUP can be an entire meal. When you are rushed, tired and drained by the day's activities and your energy is low, soup can be sustaining and satisfying. Hot soup is instant nourishment, warming to the stomach and to the soul.

With blenders and food processors to save time and labor, there isn't any reason not to make your own soup. There isn't any trick to making instant soups: Just make broth with chicken or beef bouillon cubes, boil vegetables in the broth for 5 minutes, put both liquid and vegetable into the blender after cooking, and with a whizz you have soup. Season as you please with fresh herbs, curry powder, paprika, black pepper, or white pepper—it's up to you. You will be able to control flavor, seasoning, and vitamin content when you make your own soup.

If you want to make a cold soup, frozen uncooked vegetables have a fresh garden taste and no peeling is necessary: no preparation and no waiting for the soup to chill. Just cut the frozen package open with a serrated knife, purée frozen vegetables in the blender, add the liquid of your choice—tomato juice, cream, yogurt or buttermilk—and blend until smooth. Could making soup be easier?

CELERY AND ALMOND SOUP

This pale-green creamy soup has a lovely fresh flavor; we had this soup in a Chinese restaurant in Paris.

3 cups chicken broth*
6 medium-sized inner celery stalks
10 almonds (with skins)

1. Pour broth into a saucepan, place over high heat, and boil 2 minutes.
2. Break celery stalks to remove strings; with a paring knife cut celery into small pieces into pan with broth.
3. Slowly boil celery in broth 8 minutes.
4. Pour celery and broth into a blender and purée until creamy; add almonds and chop coarsely. Serve hot in cups or small bowls.
Serves 2.

*The flavor of the chicken broth is important in this recipe as no salt or pepper is used; if you use chicken bouillon cubes, simmer 2 cubes in 3 cups of water.

VEGETABLE BROTH

2 cups chicken broth
2 tablespoons rice
1 unpeeled ripe tomato
2 unpeeled carrots
2 unpeeled zucchini
2 celery stalks, trimmed of strings
Sea salt
Freshly ground black pepper
4 parsley sprigs, chopped (no stems)

1. Bring broth to boiling in a saucepan and add rice; boil slowly 5 minutes.
2. With a chef's knife chop vegetables coarsely; add to broth and boil slowly for 5 minutes; season to taste.
3. Serve with chopped parsley sprinkled on top.
Serves 2.

PASTINA SOUP

A package of pastina (little stars or shells) from the supermarket can always be counted on to make a quick, nourishing meal, with broth and grated cheese.

4 cups chicken or beef broth
2 unpeeled zucchini
1 cup pastina
Freshly ground black pepper
Sea salt
Grated Parmesan cheese

1. Bring broth to boiling in a saucepan and simmer for 3 minutes.
2. Grate zucchini into the saucepan.
3. Add the pastina and simmer 5 minutes; season to taste.
4. Serve hot with a bowl of grated cheese.
Serves 2.

SUMMER SQUASH SOUP

A fresh-flavored soup that can be served hot or cold.

2 tablespoons unsalted butter
6 unpeeled summer squash or small zucchini
1/2 shallot, peeled
2 cups chicken broth
4 parsley sprigs (no stems)
Paprika

1. Heat butter in a saucepan; add shallot and cook 2 minutes until soft.
2. Cut thick slices of squash into pan and stir with butter and shallot.
3. Add broth to pan and bring to boil; add parsley, reduce heat, and simmer 10 minutes.
4. Purée in a blender; season with paprika to taste.
Serves 2.

CHICKEN CUSTARD IN BROTH

Preheat oven to 400°F
Have ready 4 buttered custard cups or
    tins
1 celery stalk
1/2 chicken breast, boned and skinned
3 cups chicken broth
1 egg
1/4 cup grated Parmesan cheese
4 parsley sprigs (no stems)
Sea salt
Freshly ground black pepper

1. Break celery to remove strings and cut into a blender; add chicken, 1/3 cup broth, egg, cheese, and parsley; purée until smooth.
2. With a tablespoon fill cups with purée and place cups in a pan of warm water to bake.
3. Place pan in *preheated* oven for 10 minutes.
4. Allow remaining broth to simmer while chicken custard is in the oven; season with salt and pepper to taste.
5. When custards are cooked, unmold each into a soup plate and pour hot broth into each plate; sprinkle more cheese over custard and soup. Extra chicken custard will keep in the refrigerator up to 2 days.
Makes 4 servings.

Serve with a green salad and crusty bread.

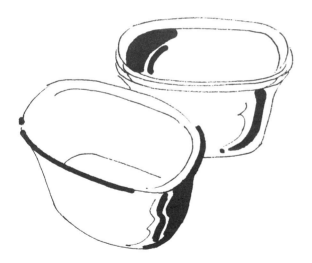

CREAMY PEA SOUP

4 cups chicken broth
4 small unpeeled new potatoes
1/2 package (about 5 ounces) frozen
  peas, or 1 cup fresh shelled peas
1/2 shallot, peeled
3 lettuce leaves
1 lemon

1. Place chicken broth in a saucepan
and bring to boil.
2. Slice potatoes into pan; add peas,
shallot, and lettuce leaves; cover pan
with a lid and simmer 10 minutes.
3. Purée soup in a blender; grate rind
of lemon into soup and serve hot.
Serves 2.

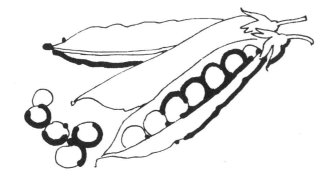

SPINACH SOUP

In Florence, Eda made this soup for us; it warmed us in the cold winter.

3 cups beef broth
10 raw spinach leaves
1/2 lemon
Grated Parmesan cheese

1. Bring broth to boiling in a saucepan; let simmer 3 minutes.
2. With a chef's knife chop spinach leaves coarsely and add to broth; squeeze in juice of lemon and cook 7 minutes.
3. Pour into bowls and serve with grated cheese.
Serves 2.

TOMATO BROTH

2 cups beef broth
2 unpeeled ripe tomatoes
1/4 cup dry white vermouth
4 parsley sprigs (no stems)
Grated rind of 1 lemon

1. Bring broth to boiling in a saucepan; reduce heat and simmer 5 minutes.
2. Slice tomatoes into pan; add vermouth, parsley, and the grated lemon rind.
3. Cook together 6 minutes.
4. Purée in a blender and serve hot.
Serves 2.

Variation Purée soup in blender; chill to serve cold; add a shot of vodka.

SHRIMP SOUP

1/4 pound raw shrimp, cleaned
1 cup half-and-half
1/4 cup dry white wine
2 teaspoons curry powder
Freshly ground white pepper

1. Combine shrimp and half-and-half in a blender; add wine and curry powder; purée.
2. Pour into a saucepan and cook over medium heat 8 minutes.
3. Season with pepper to taste; serve hot or cold.
Serves 2.

PRAWN BISQUE

1/4 pound raw prawns, cleaned
1 cup clam juice (8-ounce bottle)
1 cup heavy cream
1/4 cup dry sherry
4 parsley sprigs (no stems)
Sea salt
Freshly ground white pepper

1. Place prawns in a saucepan with clam juice and cream and bring to boil; reduce heat and simmer 3 minutes.
2. Add sherry and simmer 2 minutes.
3. Pour hot broth into a blender, add parsley, and purée.
4. Season to taste and pour into cups to serve.
Serves 2.

COLD INSTANT SOUP

Cold soups need more seasoning, as cold takes flavor away; use more paprika, pepper, salt, or herbs than you do with hot soups.

1/2 package (about 5 ounces) frozen
   green beans (or spinach, peas, or
   carrots)
1 unpeeled ripe tomato
3 cups chicken broth
1 green onion
3 parsley sprigs (no stems)
Sea salt
Freshly ground black pepper

1. Cut frozen vegetables into chunks with a serrated knife and put into blender.
2. Cut tomato into blender; add broth, green onion, and parsley.
3. Purée all together; season to taste. Serves 2.

PASTA is delicious and nutritious; it is also economical, easy to prepare, and one of the most versatile of fast foods. Low in calories, pasta has protein, vitamins, minerals, and iron, providing high energy.

The Italians prefer their pasta to be made of semolina, the finest durum wheat flour. This fine flour makes a light pasta with a firm texture and a good flavor.

Fresh pasta, cut into many widths, can be found fresh daily in Italian markets. You will find white pasta, made with eggs and flour; green pasta, made with spinach; red pasta, made with tomato; as well as tortellini and ravioli, small rounds and squares filled with ground meat and cheese.

Packaged pasta, factory-made and found on market shelves, offers a great variety in shapes and sizes: tubes, shells, butterflies, thin spaghetti, bows, corkscrews, small stars. Pasta offers as much variety in the many ways it can be cooked and served. It can be combined with vegetables, meat, or fish, and it makes an ideal base for a salad, as it absorbs sauce.

Fresh pasta must be cooked immediately, or allowed to dry; it will keep a few days refrigerated, or it can be wrapped and frozen. Packaged pastas can stay in your cupboard indefinitely.

Fresh pasta takes only a few minutes to cook in boiling water; dried pasta takes twice as long to cook; both make delicious fast meals, hot or cold with a sauce.

GREEN PASTA WITH TOMATO-CREAM SAUCE

Northern Italy: green hills dotted with red-tiled roofs, vineyards and the grey-green haze of olive groves, *trattorie* with Punt e Mes umbrellas beckon with outside tables in spring. This is pasta with the fresh tomato-cream sauce of Tuscany.

3 quarts water
4 unpeeled ripe tomatoes
6 small fresh basil leaves, or 1 teaspoon dried basil
1 cup heavy cream
Freshly ground white pepper
1/2 pound green spinach pasta
1/2 cup grated Parmesan cheese

1. Fill a large saucepan with water and place over high heat to boil for pasta.
2. Cut tomatoes into a saucepan; add basil and cook over low heat, covered, for 5 minutes.
3. Place a sieve over a bowl, pour tomatoes and basil into sieve, and press through with back of a tablespoon.
4. Bring cream to simmer in a saucepan and boil 5 minutes, stirring so it won't boil over (cream must boil to thicken). Add 1 cup sieved tomatoes to cream; season with pepper to taste.
5. Add pasta in small amounts to rapidly boiling water (if pot is too small or too much pasta is added at once, pasta will stick together). Cooking time will vary from 2–7 minutes, depending upon size, shape, and thickness of the pasta; fresh pasta will cook in 2–3 minutes.
6. When cooked, drain pasta into a colander. Don't overcook pasta; remember: It will continue to cook while draining, and pasta should be slightly firm to the bite.
7. Pour immediately into a warm bowl (if pasta cools, it will stick together) and mix with sauce. Serve with a bowl of grated cheese at table.
Serves 2.

ANGEL'S HAIR PASTA
WITH ASPARAGUS

In Venice they brought us lunch on the terrace of the hotel. The food was superb: Carpaccio, and this dish made with thin, thin coils of pasta, like an angel's hair.

3 quarts water
12 asparagus stalks
2 tablespoons unsalted butter
2 cups heavy cream
6 coils angel's hair pasta (sold in
    boxes in the supermarket)
1/2 cup grated Parmesan cheese
Freshly ground black pepper

1. Fill a large saucepan with water and put over high heat to boil for pasta.
2. Cut 3-inch pieces from tips of asparagus (the rest can be kept to make soup); then with a chef's knife, slice 3-inch tips into thin bias slices.
3. Heat butter in a sauté pan or skillet, add slices of asparagus, and stir into butter; cook for 3 minutes.
4. Pour cream into a saucepan and boil rapidly 3 minutes; cream must boil to reduce and thicken.
5. Add pasta coils to rapidly boiling water, 1 coil at a time, and cook about 3–4 minutes.
6. Drain pasta into a colander, pour into a warm bowl, and mix with hot asparagus and thickened cream. Add grated cheese and toss carefully; season to taste with pepper.
Serves 2.

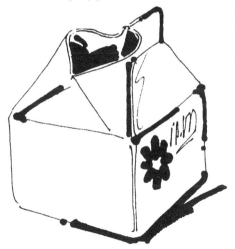

PASTA BUTTERFLIES
WITH GORGONZOLA

There is a cozy, small hotel in Milano, with each room decorated in a charming fashion; it has its own good restaurant where eating is an unqualified pleasure. I remember well the large platters of the traditional Milanese saffron risotto and beautifully presented dishes of rich pasta concoctions with white truffles and wild mushrooms; I found this delicious pasta and sauce there.

3 quarts water
1 tablespoon unsalted butter
1/4 pound Gorgonzola or Roquefort
   cheese
1 unpeeled ripe tomato
1 cup heavy cream
1/2 cup beef broth
Freshly ground black pepper
1 cup pasta butterflies (or tubes)

1. Fill a large saucepan with water and place over high heat to boil for pasta.
2. Melt butter in a sauté pan or skillet over low heat, adding cheese and mashing with a fork (cheese will melt).
3. Slice tomato into pan, crushing with a fork as it cooks; pour in cream and let boil; lower heat to simmer 4 minutes.
4. Pour in broth and simmer 3 minutes; season to taste with pepper.
5. Add pasta to rapidly boiling water and cook about 4 minutes.
6. Drain pasta into a colander and pour into a warm bowl; mix with hot sauce and serve.
Serves 2.

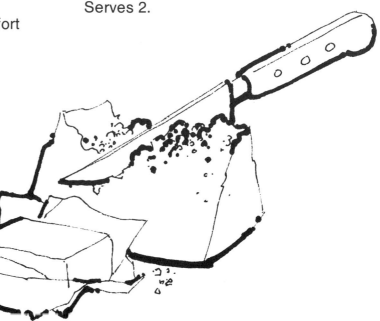

PASTA SHELLS WITH SPINACH

On Elba we drove up the winding roads through forests of chestnut to reach a small restaurant, and cooler air and the sweet smells of thyme, rosemary, oregano, and mint. In the old, quiet hilltop villages the men sit as they always have, in tree-shaded squares. The local wine we had with this pasta was light, white, and dry.

3 quarts water
2 tablespoons olive oil
2 unpeeled ripe tomatoes
30 spinach leaves (no stems or large
  tough leaves)
Sea salt
Freshly ground black pepper
1 lemon
1 cup medium-large pasta shells
1/2 cup grated Parmesan cheese

1. Fill a large saucepan with water and place over high heat to boil for pasta.
2. Warm olive oil in a sauté pan or skillet; cut tomatoes into pan and simmer 5 minutes.
3. With a chef's knife, coarsely chop spinach leaves, add to pan, and cook 5 minutes; spinach will wilt. Season with salt and pepper to taste.
4. Grate rind of lemon into pan and cook 5 minutes.
5. Add pasta to rapidly boiling water and cook about 4 minutes.
6. Drain pasta into a colander and pour pasta into a warm bowl. Mix with hot sauce. Serve a bowl of grated Parmesan cheese.
Serves 2.

Variation Thinly sliced zucchini or broccoli can be substituted for spinach.

THIN PASTA
WITH SHELLFISH AND TOMATOES

3 quarts water
4 unpeeled ripe tomatoes
2 tablespoons olive oil
4 parsley sprigs (no stems)
1/2 pound raw prawns, cleaned
Sea salt
Freshly ground black pepper
1/2 pound fresh pasta (such as *fidelini*)

1. Fill a large saucepan with water and place over high heat to boil for pasta.
2. Slice tomatoes into a blender, add oil and parsley, and purée.
3. Heat purée in a saucepan, add prawns, and simmer 5 minutes. Season to taste.
4. Add pasta to rapidly boiling water and cook for about 4 minutes.
5. Drain pasta into a colander; pour into a warm bowl and mix with hot sauce.
Serves 2.

SPAGHETTI WITH CLAMS

From Naples there is the long, magnificent view that sweeps from Vesuvius around the crescent of Naples' bay. I visited friends in their peasant kitchen with brass pots and red peppers hanging from the walls, to watch them cook this dish. We ate our meal on the terrace in the dazzling sunlight with all of Naples before us.

3 quarts water
2 tablespoons olive oil
1 shallot, peeled
1 garlic clove, peeled
1 cup dry white wine
One 6-1/2-ounce can small clams or
   mussels, or 12 fresh clams
1/2 pound thin spaghetti
Sea salt
Freshly ground white pepper

1. Fill a large saucepan with water and place over high heat to boil for pasta.
2. Warm oil in a sauté pan or skillet.
3. With a chef's knife chop shallot and garlic; add to warm oil and cook slowly, about 1 minute, until soft, not brown.
4. Pour in wine, raise heat, and cook 2 minutes to thicken.
5. Add clams and liquid from can (or washed fresh clams in shells); lower heat and cook 4 minutes.
6. Put thin strands of spaghetti into rapidly boiling water to cook 2–3 minutes.
7. Drain spaghetti into a colander, pour into a warm bowl, and mix with sauce (if clams are fresh, serve in shells).
8. Season to taste and serve hot.
Serves 2.

TORTELLINI IN BROTH

Tortellini is the king of Bolognese pasta. The small bite-sized rounds, stuffed with pork, ham, cheese, eggs, and walnuts, make a complete meal. The legend in Bologna is that a chef invented tortellini in memory of his lover's navel.

You can buy a package of frozen tortellini in a supermarket to keep in your freezer for an instant meal.

2 cups chicken broth
One 12-ounce package frozen tortellini
2 unpeeled zucchini
1/2 cup grated Parmesan cheese

1. Pour broth into a large sauté pan or skillet (so tortellini can spread out) and bring broth to boiling; reduce heat and simmer 2 minutes.

2. Add tortellini to broth and cook 3 minutes.
3. Grate zucchini into pan and simmer in broth with tortellini 2 minutes. Serve hot in bowls with grated cheese.
Serves 2.

Variation Cook tortellini in broth, drain, and serve with a sauce made of 2 cups heavy cream boiled 5 minutes until thickened and reduced; mix with grated Parmesan cheese.

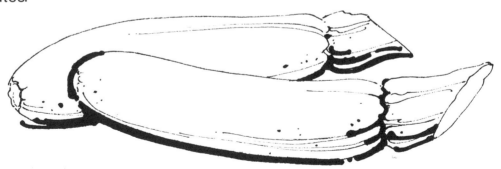

COLD PASTA SALAD

We spent one summer in St. Tropez, where we found sparkling water, sun umbrellas, hundreds of visiting yachts, and scattered houses in the hills. St. Tropez is a small village with many restaurants by the water; we had this salad nearly every day.

3 quarts water
1 cup pasta shells (holes and hollows hold the dressing)
1 egg
1/2 cup safflower oil
One 7-ounce can solid light tuna packed in olive oil (preferably imported Italian tuna)
6 anchovies
4 parsley sprigs (no stems)
1–2 lemons
2 tablespoons capers, drained
Freshly ground black pepper
8 lettuce leaves

1. Bring 3 quarts water to boiling over high heat in a large saucepan.
2. Pour shells into rapidly boiling water and cook about 5 minutes until barely soft.
3. While shells are cooking make sauce: Break egg into blender and turn on to blend quickly; slowly add oil. When oil and egg thicken, add tuna with oil from can, anchovies, and parsley.
4. Pour sauce into a bowl, squeeze in juice of lemon, stir in capers, and season with pepper to taste.
5. Drain shells into a colander and spoon into bowl with sauce; toss gently to coat pasta with sauce (this must be done while shells are hot or they will stick together).
6. Serve salad at room temperature in a bowl lined with lettuce leaves.
Serves 2.

PESTO SAUCE

This sauce is eaten by Italians with all kinds of pasta; it can also be used on a baked potato instead of butter, and is good stirred into vegetable soup.

2 garlic cloves, peeled
1 cup fresh basil leaves (no stems)
1 cup parsley sprigs (no stems)
1/2–3/4 cup olive oil
1/2 cup grated Parmesan cheese
1/4 cup pine nuts

1. Put garlic into a blender with basil and parsley; purée.
2. Start adding olive oil to this thick purée a little at a time.
3. Add cheese and pine nuts; purée; continue adding oil until finished sauce is like creamed butter, adding more oil if too thick.
Makes 1-1/2 cups.

This sauce freezes well.

HERB SAUCE FOR PASTA

4 unpeeled ripe tomatoes, or 4 canned
  tomatoes
3 celery stalks, broken to remove strings
1 tablespoon red wine vinegar
2 tablespoons olive oil
Several leaves fresh oregano, or
  1 teaspoon dried oregano
Several leaves fresh basil, or 1 teaspoon
  dried basil
2 tablespoons capers, drained
Sea salt
Freshly ground black pepper

1. Cut tomatoes and celery into a
blender and purée.
2. Add vinegar, oil, and herbs and blend.
3. Pour sauce into a bowl, add capers,
and season to taste.
Makes 1 cup.

Serve over hot cooked pasta; do not
add cheese.

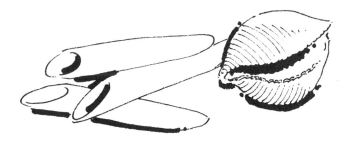

TUNA SAUCE FOR PASTA

4 unpeeled ripe tomatoes
1/4–1/2 cup olive oil
5 anchovies
10 black olives, pitted
One 7-ounce can solid light tuna,
    packed in olive oil (preferably imported
    Italian tuna)
4 parsley sprigs (no stems)

1. Slice tomatoes into a blender; add
1/4 cup oil, anchovies, and olives, and
blend to make a coarse purée.
2. Add tuna, with oil from can, and
parsley to blender; blend all together. If
too thick, add more oil.
Makes 1 cup.

UNCOOKED FRESH TOMATO SAUCE

4 unpeeled ripe tomatoes
1/2 shallot, peeled
3–4 leaves fresh basil or oregano, or
  1 teaspoon dried basil or oregano
Sea salt
Freshly ground white pepper

1. Cut tomatoes into a blender; add shallot and basil; purée.
2. When you are ready to use sauce, heat in a saucepan and season to taste.
Makes 1 cup.

Variation Put 1 cup canned peeled tomatoes, juice and all, into a blender with basil and shallot; purée. Pour purée into a pan, heat, and season to taste.
Makes 1 cup.

COOKED TOMATO SAUCE

This is a basic tomato sauce.

4 unpeeled ripe tomatoes
1/2 cup chicken or beef broth
Sea salt
Freshly ground white pepper

1. Cut tomatoes coarsely into a saucepan, add broth, and bring to boiling.
2. Lower heat to simmer, cover pan, and cook for 5–6 minutes.
3. Mash tomatoes with a tablespoon as they cook.
4. Pour tomato sauce into a sieve over a bowl and press through sieve with the back of a tablespoon.
5. When you are ready to use sauce, reheat in a saucepan and season to taste.
Makes 2 cups.

Juicy fruit-vegetables, such as tomatoes, chill well; a purée of fresh tomatoes makes an excellent iced soup, or even an ice.

MEAT SAUCE FOR PASTA

The food and cuisine of Bologna are superb; spaghettis and macaronis in all shapes are among Bologna's glories. In Bologna we had this rich, spicy sauce, and platterfuls of salami.

1 tablespoon olive oil
1/2 yellow onion, chopped
1/2 pound lean ground beef*
    (ground chuck or top round)
4 parsley sprigs, chopped (no stems)
2 unpeeled ripe tomatoes
1/2 cup dry red wine
Sea salt
Freshly ground black pepper

1. Heat oil in a sauté pan or skillet; add onion and cook 1 minute.
2. Stir in meat and parsley and cook 2–3 minutes, until meat is browned.
3. Slice tomatoes into pan, mashing them with a fork as they cook.
4. Add wine and season to taste.
5. Cover pan and cook over medium heat 10 minutes.
Serves 2.

Mix this sauce with any cooked pasta in a warm bowl; coat the hot pasta thoroughly with the sauce. Serve with a bowl of grated Parmesan cheese on the table.

*Meat should be freshly ground by your butcher or in your blender.

RICE

Imported Italian rice is the best to use for risotto dishes, as it cooks in a small amount of liquid to a perfect creamy state; never wash Italian rice. Lovely plump kernels of rice are delicious and totally satisfying when cooked and coated with butter and cheese.

RICE WITH LEMON

3 cups chicken broth
2 tablespoons unsalted butter
1 cup unwashed Italian Arborio rice
2 eggs, at room temperature
2 lemons
1/2 cup grated Parmesan cheese

1. Pour broth into a saucepan to simmer slowly while cooking rice.
2. Heat butter in a sauté pan or skillet, add rice, and stir for 1 minute until each grain of rice is coated with butter.
3. Add 1 cup hot broth, stir, and cook about 3 minutes until broth is absorbed.
4. Pour in second cup hot broth and simmer 4–5 minutes until rice is soft but firm in center; add 1/2 cup hot broth if rice needs longer cooking.
5. Whisk eggs until frothy in a bowl; add juice of lemons and cheese.
6. When rice is soft in center, stir egg mixture into rice in pan and cook over low heat 1 minute; rice should be very creamy.
Serves 2.

This makes a whole meal—you will need only a green vegetable.

SAFFRON RICE

In Milan we walked along the street famed for shopping, Via Monte Napoleone; the food store to end all food stores is there, Il Salumaio. There are fresh salads made with rice, risotto with saffron, and risotto made with four different kinds of cheese; 20 kinds of fresh pasta in colors ranging from green to orange to cocoa to white; and goat cheese wrapped in palm leaves soaking in Tuscan oil and leaves of thyme.

3 cups chicken or beef broth
2 tablespoons unsalted butter
1/2 yellow onion, finely chopped
1/4 teaspoon saffron
1/2 cup unwashed Italian Arborio rice
Sea salt

1. Pour broth into a saucepan to simmer slowly while cooking rice.
2. Heat butter in a sauté pan or skillet, stir in onion, and cook 1 minute until soft.
3. Add saffron, stirring with butter and onion.
4. Pour in rice, stirring to coat well with butter and saffron; cook about 2 minutes.
5. Pour in 1 cup hot broth and simmer until broth is absorbed, about 4–5 minutes; continue adding broth 1/2 cup at a time until rice is done, about 6–7 minutes (rice should be soft, but firm inside). Season to taste with salt.
Serves 2.

GREEN RICE

The Italians say: "Wash your hands, but never wash the rice."

3 cups chicken broth
2 tablespoons unsalted butter
1/2 shallot, peeled and chopped
1 cup unwashed Italian Arborio rice
1 cup raw spinach leaves
6 parsley sprigs (no stems)
Sea salt
Freshly ground white pepper
1/2 cup grated Parmesan cheese

1. Pour broth into a saucepan and simmer slowly while cooking rice.
2. Heat butter in a sauté pan or skillet, stir shallot into butter, and cook 1 minute.
3. Add rice; stir into butter until well coated.
4. With a chef's knife chop spinach and parsley coarsely; stir into pan; add 1 cup hot broth and cook about 3 minutes until absorbed.
5. Pour in second cup of broth and simmer 4–5 minutes until rice is tender but firm in center. If rice is hard, add hot broth 1/2 cup at a time until cooked, and season to taste.
6. Rice should be creamy and all liquid absorbed; when done, remove from heat, add grated cheese, and serve hot. Serves 2.

RICE WITH CHOPPED VEGETABLES

3 cups chicken broth
2 tablespoons unsalted butter
1/2 cup unwashed Italian Arborio rice
3 slices prosciutto
1 cup coarsely chopped vegetables
　　(3–4 spinach leaves, 1 carrot, 2 celery
　　stalks, 3–4 green beans, 1 zucchini,
　　a few fresh peas)
1/2 cup grated Parmesan cheese
Coarsely ground white pepper

1. Pour broth into a saucepan and simmer slowly while rice is cooking.
2. Heat butter in a sauté pan or skillet; add rice, stirring until each grain is coated with butter and glistens, about 2 minutes.
3. With a chef's knife slice prosciutto into thin slices and stir into pan; add vegetables, cooking together 1 minute.
4. Add 1 cup hot broth, stir, and cook for about 2 minutes, or until broth is absorbed.
5. Add second cup of hot broth and cook slowly, uncovered, over low heat about 5–6 minutes, or until rice is done. Test rice by tasting. As soon as rice is cooked but still firm in center, remove from heat. If rice is not done, add 1/2 cup hot broth and cook 3–4 minutes longer.
6. Stir in grated cheese and season to taste with pepper; serve immediately. Serves 2.

RICE WITH SHRIMP

We had this risotto in a restaurant built over the water on the island of Elba; the waiter takes the fish out of the sea while you watch, and it is cooked for you in minutes. Elba has a brilliant sky filled with beautiful birds; the island is surrounded by clear blue water filled with fish and jutting rocks.

1 cup water
1 cup hot clam juice (8-ounce bottle)
2 tablespoons unsalted butter
1 garlic clove, peeled and halved
1/2 pound raw shrimp, cleaned
2 tablespoons brandy
1/2 cup unwashed Italian Arborio rice
Sea salt
Freshly ground white pepper

1. Pour water and clam juice into a saucepan to simmer slowly while rice is cooking.
2. Heat butter in a sauté pan or skillet, add garlic, and cook, stirring, for 1 minute.
3. Stir shrimp into pan with butter and garlic.
4. Pour brandy into pan, ignite, and stir when flames die; remove garlic with a spoon.
5. Stir rice into pan and cook 2 minutes until well coated and glistening.
6. Pour 1 cup hot broth into pan and simmer slowly until broth is absorbed, about 3–4 minutes.
7. Add second cup of hot broth and cook rice slowly until it is tender but firm inside. Season to taste. Take to table to serve hot.
Serves 2.

FISH is the perfect fast food. Don't be lazy about cooking fish; in minutes you can have moist and tender fish to eat.

There is a variety of fish to suit your taste; you will see them all glittering on ice in a well-stocked fish market: the seasonal fish and shellfish with appealing tastes and textures; the solid white fish such as red snapper, swordfish, halibut, and sea bass; the oily and more flavorful fish such as mackerel, sardines, and salmon.

Very fresh fish, smelling of the sea, with bright eyes and firm flesh, is lovely to see and easy to cook. There are endless methods of preparing fresh fish—broiling, sautéing, baking, steaming, poaching—all methods are simple; you can have a delicious meal in minutes. All you must do is remember: More often than not fish is ruined by overcooking.

Tomatoes, oil, onions, garlic, and aromatic herbs are used in cooking fish in Italy and in the south of France. Green peas, mushrooms, watercress, celery, and cucumber go well with fish, as do fennel, mint, tarragon, and basil. Use your imagination in making your own combinations of vegetables and herbs to add flavor and color to your fish dishes.

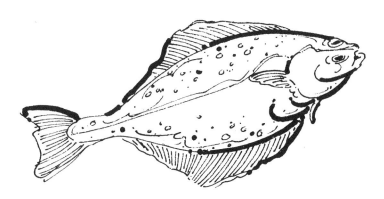

SOLE WITH MUSHROOMS

Baste thin slices of firm, fresh, pink-white sole with olive oil and lemon juice while cooking in the oven; it is so easy. Sole fillets take only a few minutes to cook; don't use frozen ones, as the flavor and texture are not the same.

Preheat oven to 375°F
4 fillets of sole
1/2 pound raw shrimp or prawns, cleaned
2 tablespoons unsalted butter
8 unpeeled mushrooms
1 glass white wine
Sea salt
Freshly ground white pepper
Paprika

1. Lay fillets in a baking dish and surround with the shellfish.
2. Sprinkle bits of butter over sole and into dish.
3. Slice mushrooms over sole; pour wine into dish.
4. Place in *preheated* oven 3–4 minutes. When butter has melted, baste fish and mushrooms and season to taste.
5. Return to oven to cook 5–6 minutes; baste again. When done the fish will flake easily when tested with a fork.
6. Remove fish from oven and serve with sauce from pan.
Serves 2.

FISH WITH MUSTARD SAUCE

In Venice I was fascinated by the food market at the edge of the Grand Canal. Almost every dawn I went to see the fish and vegetable stalls. The fishermen decorate their morning catch with lemons, bright green peas and plums, blue cabbages, ruby-red beets, and orange zucchini flowers, as they display the fish in the stalls. The rosy-gold light of the Venetian dawn makes the vegetables and fruit seem as exotic as the fish. Even ordinary fish are bright with color: sole striped with delicate lilac lights; glistening silver sardines; and pink, fat scampi.

Preheat oven to 425°F
1/2 pound white fish, boned and skinned
1/4 pound raw prawns, cleaned (leave tails on)
1/2 cup dry white wine
2 tablespoons olive oil
6 parsley sprigs (no stems)
1 small shallot, peeled
1 tablespoon Dijon mustard
Sea salt
Freshly ground black pepper

1. Cut fish into two pieces and place in a baking dish. Sprinkle prawns around fish.
2. Combine wine, oil, parsley, shallot, and mustard in a blender; purée. Pour purée over fish and prawns.
3. Place baking dish in *preheated* oven to bake 10–12 minutes, basting twice while fish is cooking; season to taste. Serves 2.

WHITE FISH WITH ORANGE SLICES

I had fish cooked with oranges in Sicily; in the 18th century oranges were used for flavoring fish as lemons are today.

2 tablespoons unsalted butter
4 thin slices sole or halibut
2 oranges
1/2 cup white wine
Sea salt
Freshly ground white pepper
1/2 bunch watercress

1. Heat butter until foaming in a sauté pan or skillet; add fish and cook about 1 minute on each side (they will cook quickly).
2. Remove fish to a warm plate, squeeze juice of 1 orange into pan, and stir bottom of pan to scrape cooked bits into sauce.
3. Slice 4 thin slices from orange (un-peeled) and add to pan.
4. Pour white wine into pan with orange slices and cook over medium heat 3 minutes.
5. Return fish to pan, spoon sauce over fish, and cook 1 minute. Season to taste. Garnish with cooked orange slices and watercress. Take pan to table to serve sauce over fish.
Serves 2.

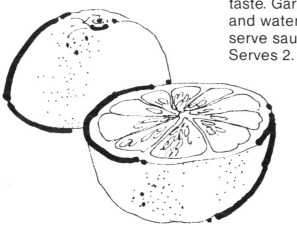

HALIBUT WITH TOMATOES AND BLACK OLIVES

Halibut is my favorite white fish because of its flavor and firm texture.

Preheat oven to 375°F
2 pieces halibut (1/2 pound), boned
   and skinned
1/4 cup olive oil
2 unpeeled ripe tomatoes
8–10 black olives (preferably Italian,
   Greek, or Provençal for flavor)
1 tablespoon chopped fresh oregano,
   or 2 teaspoons dried oregano
1/2 cup white wine
Sea salt
Freshly ground black pepper

1. Arrange fish in a baking dish and pour oil over fish.
2. Slice tomatoes into dish around fish; sprinkle olives and oregano over fish and tomatoes.
3. Place dish in *preheated* oven and bake 7–8 minutes.
4. Pour wine into dish; with a tablespoon, baste fish with pan juices and wine. Season to taste.
5. Bake 5–6 minutes; baste again and test fish with a fork (fish will flake when done).
Serves 2.

This is good with spinach and simply boiled rice.

BAKED SALMON

Preheat oven to 400°F
2 salmon fillets (1/2 pound), boned and skinned
1/2 cup heavy cream
5 branches fresh tarragon, or 1 table-spoon dried tarragon
Freshly ground black pepper.

1. Lay salmon flat in an oven dish and pour cream over salmon.
2. Surround fillets with branches of tarragon, or sprinkle dried tarragon over salmon; season to taste with pepper.
3. Bake in *preheated* oven 10–12 minutes; baste twice while salmon is cooking.
Serves 2.

SALMON WITH WHITE WINE

1 tablespoon unsalted butter
1 small shallot, peeled and chopped
2 salmon steaks or fillets (1/2 pound)
1/2 cup white wine
Sea salt
Freshly ground black pepper
4 parsley sprigs, chopped (no stems)
1 lemon, halved

1. Melt butter in sauté pan or skillet over low heat; add shallot and stir until soft, about 1 minute.
2. Add salmon to pan and cook in butter 1 minute on each side.
3. Pour wine into pan, cover pan and cook 6 minutes.
4. Season to taste; sprinkle parsley over fish. Take pan to table to serve salmon with sauce from pan; garnish with lemon halves.
Serves 2.

BAKED WHITE FISH

Preheat oven to 400°F
2 pieces white fish (1/4 pound per person) such as swordfish, red snapper, or sea bass
1/4 cup olive oil
2 small inner celery stalks or fennel stalks
1/2 yellow onion
1 unpeeled ripe tomato
1/4 cup grated Parmesan cheese
1/2 cup white wine
Sea salt
Freshly ground black pepper
1 lemon, cut into quarters

1. Lay fish in an oven dish and dribble oil over fish.
2. With a chef's knife coarsely chop celery and onion and place both around fish in dish.
3. Slice tomato into dish over fish; sprinkle cheese over fish and vegetables.
4. Place dish in *preheated* oven and cook 5 minutes. Pour wine into bottom of dish and baste fish; season to taste.
5. Return dish to oven, cook 5–6 minutes, and baste again. Fish should flake when done. Garnish with quartered lemon and serve.
Serves 2.

POACHED FISH

Serve your poached fish with a separate sauce; put some small new potatoes on to boil, as they, too, can be eaten with the sauce. Serve poached fish at room temperature, not hot.

8 cups water
1 carrot
1 celery stalk
1 bay leaf
4 peppercorns
1/2 cup white wine, or juice of 1 lemon
1/2 pound salmon, or any white fish

1. Heat water to boiling in a saucepan; cut carrot and celery into pan; add bay leaf, peppercorns, and wine; boil slowly 5 minutes.
2. Reduce heat under pan to simmer and add fish (do not boil fish, or it will break).
3. Cook fish in gently simmering water 5 minutes (fish is done as soon as it flakes when tested with a fork).
4. Remove fish from water with a slotted spoon and place on a plate to cool.
Serves 2.

Serve with Aioli, Tarragon, or Yogurt Sauce; this is an elegant meal with small potatoes, a green vegetable, and a glass of white wine.

BROILED FISH ON SKEWERS

Preheat broiler at full broil
1/2 pound firm white fish, such as
  halibut
3 tablespoons olive oil
2 lemons
1 shallot, peeled
8–10 bay leaves

1. Cut fish into small squares and put into a bowl.
2. Pour olive oil over fish and squeeze juice of 1 lemon into bowl. Cut shallot into bowl and let fish sit in mixture for 5 minutes.
3. Thread fish squares and bay leaves alternately on thin wooden skewers. Place skewers on an oven sheet and put under *preheated* broiler, about 5 minutes.
4. Baste fish 2–3 times while cooking, and turn skewers as fish colors. Serve immediately, with quartered lemon. Serves 2.

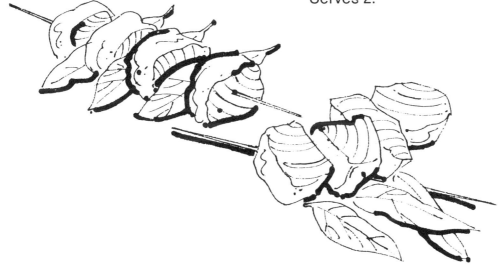

SAUTEED PRAWNS

The great musical treat in Venice is the Fenice, surely the prettiest opera house in Europe, with its interior of red plush and gilt. At the restaurant next door we had the perfect pre-theatre snack.

1 tablespoon olive oil
2 teaspoons dried basil
1 shallot, peeled and chopped
1/2 pound raw prawns, cleaned (leave tails on)
1 lemon
Sea salt
Freshly ground black pepper
6 parsley sprigs, chopped (no stems)

1. Heat oil in a sauté pan or skillet; add basil to warm in the oil; add shallot and cook over low heat until soft, not brown.
2. Stir prawns into pan and cook with shallot and basil 5 minutes over low heat (prawns will turn pink as they cook).
3. Squeeze lemon juice into pan over prawns.
4. Season to taste and sprinkle parsley over prawns; take to table to serve in pan.
Serves 2.

FISH SOUP

After visiting the Picasso Museum in the Grimaldi Palace in old Antibes, we walked to a restaurant near the sea. There we had this hearty soup made with fresh fish from the bluest sea I have ever seen.

2 unpeeled ripe tomatoes
1/2 yellow onion
1 garlic clove, peeled
6 parsley sprigs (no stems)
2 tablespoons olive oil
1 bay leaf
1 cup clam juice (8-ounce bottle)
1 cup water
1/2 pound white fish fillets (halibut, cod, or red snapper)
1 cup white wine
Sea salt
Freshly ground black pepper

1. Cut tomato and onion into a blender, add garlic and parsley, and blend to a coarse texture.
2. Heat oil in a large saucepan with bay leaf; stir in vegetables from blender and cook 2 minutes.
3. Pour in clam juice and water and bring to boil; remove bay leaf with a tablespoon.
4. Add fish to pan and simmer 5 minutes; as fish cooks, break it into small pieces with a tablespoon.
5. Pour wine into pan and simmer 4 minutes. Season to taste and stir well. Serves 2.

Serve soup hot in bowls with crusty bread, a piece of cheese, and a bowl of Aioli on the table.

SCALLOPS

The best fish restaurant in Cannes is noisy and always so crowded the waiters must carry the trays high in the air in order to pass the tables. Here you can find broiled fish with fennel; fish stew with garlic, tomatoes, anchovies, and brandy; fresh sardines; and fresh scallops. The scallops in this restaurant are served in large scallop shells, with the sauce bubbling and brown from the broiler.

2 tablespoons unsalted butter
1 shallot, peeled and chopped
1/2 cup heavy cream
1/2 pound scallops
Paprika
1/4 cup dry white vermouth
4 parsley sprigs, chopped (no stems)

1. Melt butter in a sauté pan or skillet; add shallot and stir until soft, about 1 minute.
2. Pour in cream, raise heat, and boil for 2 minutes.
3. Add scallops and cook slowly 2–3 minutes.
4. Season with paprika to taste; add vermouth and cook 1 minute longer.
5. Sprinkle with parsley and serve. Serves 2.

CRAB LEGS SAUTE

2 tablespoons unsalted butter
1 small shallot, peeled
6 unpeeled mushrooms
8 fresh crab legs, or one 6-1/2-ounce
   can crab legs, drained
1/2 cup dry white vermouth or white
   wine
Freshly ground white pepper

1. Melt butter over medium heat in a
sauté pan or skillet.
2. With a chef's knife chop shallot very
fine and add to pan to cook in butter
until soft.
3. Wash mushrooms and slice thinly
into pan, mixing with shallots and butter;
cook 1 minute.
4. Add crab legs, stir with butter and
vegetables, and cook 2 minutes.
5. Pour wine into pan and simmer
uncovered over low heat 4 minutes.
Season with pepper to taste and take
pan to table to serve hot.
Serves 2.

SAUCES FOR FISH

AIOLI

A garlic mayonnaise.

1 egg
1/2–3/4 cup oil
2 garlic cloves, peeled
1/2 unpeeled ripe tomato
1 lemon
Sea salt
Freshly ground black pepper

1. Break egg into blender and turn on
blender to mix quickly; add oil in a thin
stream until egg and oil thicken.
2. Add garlic cloves; purée, then
add tomato; if too thin, add more oil.
3. Squeeze juice of lemon into blender
and mix well.
4. Pour sauce from blender into a bowl;
season to taste.
Makes 1-1/2 cups.

TARRAGON SAUCE

1 egg
1/2–3/4 cup oil
4 branches fresh tarragon (leaves only),
   or 2 teaspoons dried tarragon
1 lemon
Sea salt
Freshly ground black pepper

1. Break egg into blender and turn on blender to mix quickly; add oil in a thin stream until egg and oil thicken.
2. Add tarragon, squeeze juice of lemon into blender, and blend all together.
3. Pour sauce from blender into a bowl; season to taste.
Makes about 1 cup.

YOGURT SAUCE

1 cup plain yogurt
1 unpeeled ripe tomato
1/2 shallot, peeled
1 lemon
Dash Tabasco sauce

1. Place yogurt in a blender, cut tomato into blender, add shallot, and purée.
2. Squeeze juice of lemon into blender, add Tabasco, and mix well together.
Makes 1 cup.

HORSERADISH SAUCE

1/2 cup mayonnaise
1/2 cup sour cream
2 tablespoons horseradish (bottled)
1 lemon

1. Place mayonnaise, sour cream, and horseradish in a bowl and stir well to mix.
2. Squeeze juice of lemon into bowl and blend all contents together.
Makes 1 cup.

BASIL BUTTER

Good with fish or pasta.

1/4 pound (1/2 cup) unsalted butter
1/2 cup fresh basil leaves, or 1 tablespoon dried basil
Sea salt
Freshly ground black pepper

1. Melt butter in a small sauté pan or
skillet, add basil leaves, and cook together 1 minute.
2. Pour butter and basil into a blender
and purée.
3. Pour into a small bowl, season to
taste, and serve warm.
Makes 1/2 cup.

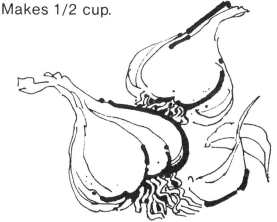

FENNEL BUTTER

From the wild-herb–scented fields of
Provence come meals of wonderful
herb-flavored fish and lamb, herb butters,
and pink Provençal wines.

1/4 pound (1/2 cup) unsalted butter
6 teaspoons fennel seeds
1/2 garlic clove, peeled and chopped
1 lemon
Sea salt
Freshly ground black pepper

1. Melt butter in a small sauté pan or
skillet, add fennel seeds, and cook 1
minute.
2. Stir in garlic and cook 1 minute,
stirring so garlic does not brown.
3. Squeeze juice of lemon into pan and
cook 1 minute, stirring all together;
season to taste.
Makes 1/2 cup.

CHICKEN has a hundred different personalities: Chicken can be flavored with herbs and vegetables, made spicy cooked with curry or bland with cream; it loves fresh lemon, orange, basil and thyme, parsley and rosemary. Chicken can be colored with saffron, tarragon, tomato, or mustard. Cut into small pieces, chicken is a fast food: It can be broiled; poached in broth, wine, or orange juice; served in a delicate pale-green tarragon sauce or a red tomato sauce spiked with black olives. Chicken likes to be cooked with mixtures of aromatic vegetables. Chicken breasts can be sliced thin, rolled in bread crumbs or cheese; sautéed with shallots and butter; stuffed with pâté or truffles.

Try the endless variety of ways chicken can be cooked, all easy and delicious.

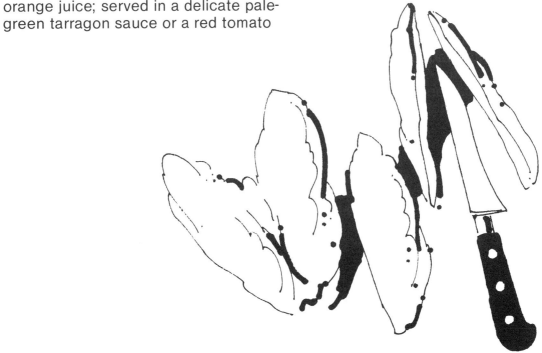

HOW TO BONE A CHICKEN BREAST

Instead of paying a premium price for boned chicken breasts, take your boning knife and chicken breast in hand, slip the sharp point of the knife under the flesh and cut along the bone, lifting the chicken flesh as you cut. When breast meat is released from the bone, slip the knife between skin and flesh, and carefully cut off the skin. You will have the bones and skin to put into the pan for a rich broth.

No one these days can afford to waste food; often people waste good food because they do not understand the sport of economy. It becomes a game to make everything count: Bone and skin chicken breasts and use bones and skin for broth; use leftover cooked scraps to fill crêpes, omelets, and soufflés. Use every bit of food—every lettuce leaf, vegetable skin, and fruit peel—to enrich and flavor your cooking.

MAKE A RICH BROTH FROM SCRAPS OF CHICKEN

Chicken makes a flavorful and useful broth for cooking. Using a clear fat-free broth as a cooking liquid will improve the flavor of soups and sauces. Many dishes depend on a good broth; substitutes, though quick and easy, are not the same. Whenever you trim fat or skin from a piece of chicken or bone a chicken breast, put trimmings (bones, skin, fat) aside for broth; put all into a plastic bag in your freezer, if you are not ready to use them.

To make broth, put bones, skin, fat, scraps into a saucepan and cover with water (just cover with water, add no more), bring to boil, and simmer rapidly 15 minutes. Pour into a sieve, strain into a bowl, and refrigerate until the fat congeals and can be removed. You will have a better broth in this short time than you can buy, as commercial broths are highly seasoned.

CHICKEN WITH CHUTNEY

Preheat oven to 450°F
2 whole chicken breasts, halved, boned,
  and skinned
1/2 cup mayonnaise
1/2 cup sour cream
2 tablespoons chutney
1 teaspoon curry powder
1 lemon
Freshly ground black pepper

1. Lay 4 pieces of chicken flat in an
oven dish.
2. Combine mayonnaise and sour cream
in a bowl. Stir in chutney and curry
powder and squeeze in juice of lemon.
3. Cover chicken with this sauce, place
in *preheated* hot oven, and bake 12
minutes. Season with pepper to taste.
Take dish to table to serve hot.
Serves 2.

This exotic dish is good with Couscous
Salad.

CHICKEN WITH CHOPPED CELERY AND FENNEL

I had this dish in a restaurant in the tiny
village of Mougins in the hills above
Cannes on the Côte d'Azur. The restaurant is tucked into a hillside grove of
trees and flowers, overlooking the
Mediterranean.

1 tablespoon unsalted butter
2 teaspoons green peppercorns in
  vinegar
1 whole chicken breast, halved, boned,
  and skinned
1 cup chopped celery
1 cup chopped fennel (use a total of
  2 cups chopped celery if fennel is
  not available)
1 cup chicken broth

1. Melt butter in a sauté pan or skillet, add green peppercorns, and stir 1 minute.
2. Place chicken in pan and cook over medium heat until tan, about 2 minutes on each side.
3. Add celery and fennel to sides of pan with chicken in center.
4. Pour in 1/2 cup chicken broth, cover pan with a piece of heavy brown bag paper cut in a circle to fit over pan, and simmer over low heat 7 minutes.

5. Add remaining 1/2 cup of broth to pan, raise heat, and boil rapidly 2 minutes to reduce and thicken sauce. Serve chicken garnished with vegetables and sauce.
Serves 2.

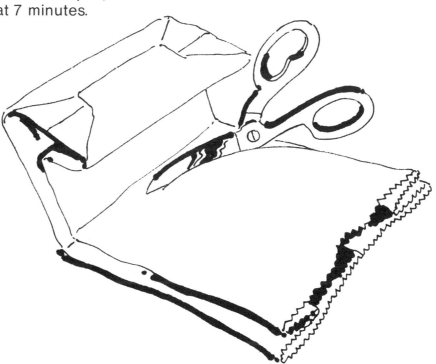

TUSCAN CHICKEN

If you cut a whole chicken into small pieces it will cook quickly, and you will have many possibilities for a variety of recipes. Legs and thighs can be broiled or baked, breasts can be sauced, and the back and bony parts can be used for broth.

2 tablespoons unsalted butter
8 chicken thighs
1/4 cup brandy
1 unpeeled ripe tomato
6 unpeeled mushrooms
1/2 cup dry white wine
Sea salt
Freshly ground black pepper
4 parsley sprigs, chopped (no stems)

1. Heat butter to foaming in a sauté pan or skillet over medium heat. Add thighs and cook about 6 minutes, turning as they brown. Add brandy.
2. Slice tomato into pan (to catch all juice) and stir. Slice mushrooms into pan and cook over medium heat 5 minutes.
3. Pour wine into pan, raise heat, and cook 2 minutes to thicken sauce.
4. Season to taste; sprinkle chopped parsley over chicken and serve.
Serves 2.

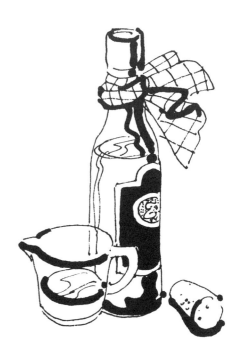

CHICKEN WITH PROSCIUTTO AND CHEESE

Lunch at Harry's Bar in Florence with a Bellini to drink, delicious toasts of fried bread, chicken with prosciutto and cheese, and *tagliarini verdi*.

1 whole chicken breast, halved, boned, and skinned
1/4 cup grated Parmesan cheese
2 tablespoons unsalted butter
4 slices prosciutto
4 slices Monterey Jack cheese
1 cup dry champagne or dry white wine
Freshly ground black pepper

1. Slice halves of chicken breast lengthwise, making 4 pieces.
2. Put grated cheese on a piece of waxed paper and roll chicken in cheese to cover both sides.
3. Heat butter to foaming in a sauté pan or skillet, add chicken, and cook until golden brown, about 2 minutes on each side.
4. Lay a slice of prosciutto and a slice of cheese (cut to fit) on each strip of chicken, and secure with a toothpick.
5. Cover pan and cook 2 minutes, or until cheese has melted; remove chicken to a warm plate.
6. Pour in wine, turn up heat, scrape pan with a tablespoon to catch all cooked bits, and boil 1 minute.
7. Serve sauce with chicken; season with pepper to taste.
Serves 2.

If you cook green beans while chicken is sautéing, you will have a complete meal.

POACHED CHICKEN WITH TARRAGON

3 cups chicken broth
1 whole chicken breast, halved, boned,
   and skinned
1 cup heavy cream
Leaves from 5–6 branches fresh
   tarragon, or 1 tablespoon dried
   tarragon
Sea salt
Freshly ground white pepper
Extra tarragon leaves for garnish

1. Bring broth to boil in a saucepan.
2. Cut chicken breasts in half lengthwise
to make 4 strips; add to broth and
simmer 6 minutes.
3. Boil cream and tarragon in a saucepan 3–4 minutes to thicken cream;
sauce will be a pale green color.
4. Add poached chicken to boiling sauce
and cook 2 minutes; season to taste.
Serve garnished with tarragon.
Serves 2.

CHICKEN WITH BROCCOLI

1 whole chicken breast, halved, boned,
  and skinned
1 egg yolk
3/4 cup chicken broth
3 tablespoons grated Parmesan cheese
2 tablespoons unsalted butter
3 broccoli stalks
Sea salt
Freshly ground black pepper
1 lemon, cut into quarters

1. Slice chicken breasts (2 halves) into
4 lengthwise strips.
2. Beat yolk in a bowl with 2 tablespoons chicken broth, add grated cheese,
and stir together.

3. Coat pieces of chicken with this egg
batter.
4. Heat butter to foaming in a sauté
pan or skillet, add chicken strips, and
cook over medium heat until golden on
all sides, about 4 minutes.
5. With a chef's knife cut tops from
broccoli (2-inch flowerettes) and chop
coarsely.
6. Remove chicken from pan to a warm
dish; put broccoli into pan over medium
heat, stir in remaining chicken broth,
and catch all cooked bits in pan with
your spoon. Cook broccoli about 5
minutes. Season to taste.
7. Place chicken and broccoli together
on plates. Pour sauce from pan over
broccoli and garnish with quartered
lemon.
Serves 2.

CHICKEN WITH PLUM SAUCE

Preheat oven to 475°F
1 pound chicken wings
1 tablespoon safflower oil
1/2 shallot, peeled
1/2 cup plum jam
1 small piece fresh ginger, peeled,
   or 1 teaspoon powdered ginger
1 tablespoon soy sauce
1 teaspoon Dijon mustard
1 orange

1. With a boning knife, cut wing tips off chicken wings (place tips in a plastic bag in the freezer to save for broth). Put wings in an oven dish.
2. Blend oil, shallot, jam, ginger, soy sauce, and mustard in a blender. Squeeze juice of orange into blender and mix all together.
3. Pour marinade sauce over chicken, turning chicken well in sauce to coat all sides.
4. Place dish in *preheated* hot oven and cook 10 minutes.
Serves 2.

The chicken and sauce go well with plain boiled rice.

GOLDEN CRISP TURKEY

Living in Italy, I became devoted to thin slices of turkey breast rolled in cheese or bread crumbs and served with lemon.

1/2 small turkey breast, boned and
   skinned (about 2 pounds)
1 egg yolk
3 tablespoons water
Dash Tabasco sauce
1 thin slice bread
1/2 teaspoon dried sage
1/2 teaspoon dried oregano
1 tablespoon unsalted butter
1 tablespoon safflower oil
Sea salt
Freshly ground black pepper
1 lemon, halved

1. With a sharp knife cut breast into 10–12 lengthwise strips.
2. Mix egg yolk in a small bowl with water and Tabasco.
3. Blend bread and herbs in a blender to make herbed bread crumbs; pour into a dish.
4. Dip strips of turkey into egg, then into herbed bread crumbs.
5. Heat butter and oil in a sauté pan or skillet. Add turkey and cook over medium heat 2 minutes, turning pieces as they become golden.
6. Season to taste; garnish with lemon halves and serve.
Serves 2.

MARINADE SAUCE
FOR SQUAB OR CHICKEN

This sauce makes fowl moist and delicious.

Preheat oven to 475°F
1 squab (about 1 pound), or 6 chicken
   legs
1/4 cup safflower oil
1/2 cup white wine
1 tablespoon Dijon mustard
3 tablespoons red currant jelly
1 lemon

1. With a boning knife cut squab in half and place skin side up in an oven dish.
2. Put oil, wine, mustard, and jelly in a small pan and squeeze in juice of lemon. Place pan over medium heat and bring contents to boil, stirring well until jelly has melted and all ingredients have blended.
3. Pour sauce over squab in dish and turn squab to coat all sides with sauce.
5. Place dish in *preheated* oven to cook 10 minutes, basting 3–4 times and turning squab as it colors.
6. Turn on broiler and place squab skin side up under broiler for 2 minutes.
Serves 2.

Serve with cucumbers sliced thin, and boiled rice mixed with grated lemon rind.

MUSTARD-ORANGE MARINADE
FOR CHICKEN AND SQUAB

Chicken and squab take to the flavors
of exotic marinades and sauces. Both
cook quickly, but take care to see
pieces are cooked through, as raw
joints are unappealing.

Preheat oven to 450°F
1/2 cup safflower oil
1/4 cup honey
Grated rind and juice of 1 orange
1 tablespoon Dijon mustard
2 teaspoons soy sauce
4 chicken legs and thighs, or one
   1-pound squab
Sea salt
Freshly ground black pepper
1 head butter lettuce, separated into
   leaves

1. Combine oil, honey, orange rind,
orange juice, mustard, and soy sauce in
a small sauté pan or skillet and heat
slowly, stirring to mix well; cook for 1
minute or until all is melted together.
2. With a chef's knife cut chicken legs
and thighs in half crosswise and put
into an oven dish.
3. Pour marinade sauce over chicken,
turning pieces to coat all sides well.
4. Place dish in preheated oven and
bake 12 minutes, basting twice while
chicken is cooking; season to taste.
Serve chicken on a plate with leaves of
butter lettuce, pouring marinade from
pan over lettuce.
Serves 2.

MEAT can be cooked in minutes when your energy and time are at a premium. The most tender cuts require only broiling or quick sautéing; they can be sliced thin (veal and pork), cooked briefly and served rare (beef and lamb).

Buy meat of the best quality. I go to a butcher where from experience I know I can depend upon the quality and the proper cutting and trimming of the meat.

To prevent spoilage and waste, refrigerate your meat properly. Meat should be removed from the butcher's paper and loosely wrapped; it should never be kept in airtight containers. Plan to use the most perishable cuts such as ground beef first (it is best to grind your own), as meat in larger pieces can be kept safely for several days. Fillets of veal, pork, and beef can be wrapped in waxed paper and frozen; they can be sliced thin when ready to use; this will be an economy in the long run.

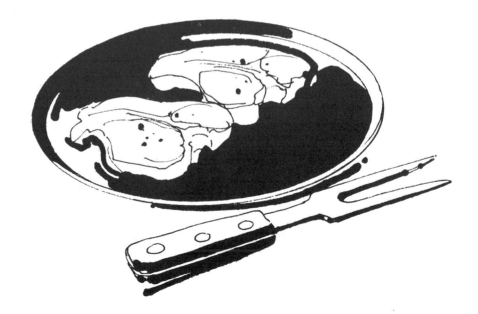

CARPACCIO

At Harry's Bar in Florence, I often had Carpaccio, named for one of the great painters of the Venetian school. Have your butcher slice the beef as thin as possible, almost transparent. Only prime beef such as filet mignon should be used, and all fat should be trimmed away. If you keep a fillet strip in the freezer it is easy to slice thin when frozen.

8 thin slices raw prime beef
2 tablespoons capers, drained
3 anchovies
4 parsley sprigs (no stems)
3 tablespoons olive oil
Dash of Worcestershire sauce
Dash of Tabasco sauce

1. Trim any fat from beef slices.
2. Put all remaining ingredients into blender for a second to blend well.
3. With a spatula, spread a thin layer of sauce on a plate; lay beef slices on sauce. Serve with more sauce in a bowl, and warm bread, a green salad, and a light red wine.
Serves 2.

Variation: In Verona I had Carpaccio with a homemade mayonnaise mixed with mustard and capers.

PAN-BROILED STEAK

I learned in Florence to cook meat simply, encouraging the flavors of the ingredients to become a delicious sauce. Cooked this way, steak will be more moist than when grilled.

1/2 pound fillet of beef (for 2 people)
3 tablespoons green or black
  peppercorns
1/4 cup dry white wine
1/4 cup beef broth
1/4 cup brandy

1. With a sharp knife trim any fat from fillet and cut in half crosswise. Press peppercorns into both sides of fillets.
2. Heat a sauté pan or skillet over high heat; put meat in pan (it will sear on bottom, forming a crust).
3. Lower heat and cook 3–4 minutes on each side, depending on the rareness desired.
4. When fillets are done, remove to a warm dish. Add wine and broth to pan and boil rapidly with pan juices 1 minute. Add brandy and cook over high heat 1 minute. Pour pan juices over fillets and serve.
Serves 2.

Mustard Sauce Variation After adding brandy to pan, stir in 1 teaspoon Dijon mustard and 4 tablespoons heavy cream. Cook 2 minutes over high heat, pour over fillets, and serve.

ITALIAN MEATBALLS

Meatballs are easy to make, but the meat must be freshly ground by your butcher or in your blender or food processor. The addition of bread, egg, and cheese makes these meatballs crusty and moist.

1/2 pound freshly ground or whole
  beef (chuck, top round, sirloin)
2 tablespoons grated Parmesan cheese
1 egg
One 3-inch piece lemon peel
1 very thin slice fresh bread
1 garlic clove, peeled
4 parsley sprigs (no stems)
Sea salt
Freshly ground black pepper
2 tablespoons olive oil

1. Put ground beef into a blender or cut meat into 3 or 4 pieces and put into blender; add cheese, egg, and lemon peel; chop coarsely.
2. Add bread, garlic, and parsley to blender and quickly blend with meat.
3. Put meat in a bowl and season to taste. Form meat into small balls about 1 inch in diameter.
4. Heat oil in a sauté pan or skillet; when oil is hot, add meatballs and cook slowly over low-medium heat 3–4 minutes, turning as they become brown and crusty.
Serves 2.

BROILED LAMB CHOPS

The trick to broiling meat is having the meat at room temperature and the oven blazing hot. I like to use my round heavy steel oven sheet for broiling chops and small steaks: Put the oven sheet under the broiler and allow to heat while oven is preheating; the sheet will be so hot it will sear the meat when it is placed on the sheet, sealing in all juices and making a thick crust.

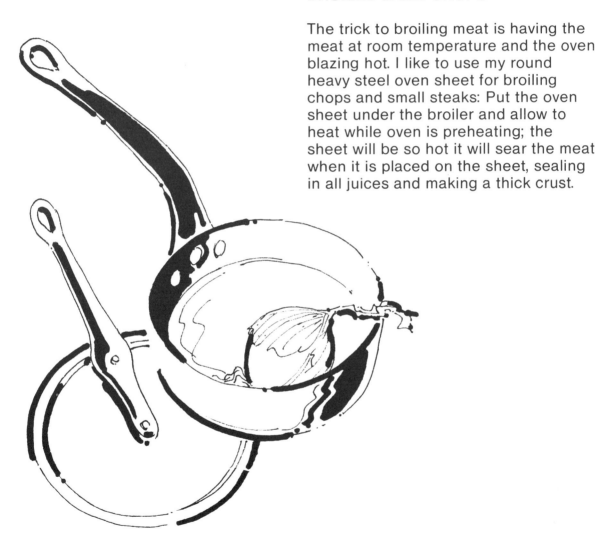

Preheat oven at full broil
Place oven sheet in oven to heat
2 lamb chops, 2–3 inches thick
4 tablespoons (1/4 cup) soft unsalted
  butter
1 tablespoon dried tarragon or
  rosemary
Sea salt
Freshly ground black pepper

1. Remove all fat from chops. With a sharp knife, make a pocket in each chop by slitting meat in thickest part of the chop.
2. Cream butter, tarragon, and salt and pepper to taste, and stuff pocket of each chop. Close chop with a toothpick.
3. Place chops on hot, preheated oven sheet under *preheated* broiler to cook for about 3 minutes; turn to broil other side for 2–3 minutes if you like them pink inside, longer if well done.
4. Serve chops with remaining herb butter on top.
Serves 2.

PAN-BROILED LAMB CHOPS

Lamb chops can be good when they are pan cooked, if done properly.

Two 1-inch-thick lamb rib chops
Sea salt
Freshly ground black pepper
2 tablespoons brandy

1. Trim lamb chops, cutting away all fat with a sharp knife.
2. Heat a sauté pan or skillet and rub it with some of the fat trimmed from the chops.
3. Place chops in hot pan (the hot pan will sear the surface, making a crust). Turn chops only once (about 2 minutes on each side) and season at the last minute.
4. Remove chops to a warm plate, pour brandy into pan, and light with a match; the alcohol will take away any fat and leave a wonderful flavor. Stir all juices together, scraping pan. Pour juice over chops and serve hot.
Serves 2.

GROUND LAMB PATTIES

You will find fresh ground lamb in most butcher shops, or you can grind a small piece of shoulder or leg in your blender or food processor.

Preheat oven to 475°F
Place oven sheet in oven to heat
1 unpeeled ripe tomato
1/2 shallot, peeled
4 parsley sprigs (no stems)
1 teaspoon dried oregano
1/2 pound ground lamb
Sea salt
Freshly ground black pepper

1. Cut tomato into a blender. Add shallot, parsley, and oregano; purée.
2. Put ground lamb in a bowl and mix in purée. Season to taste and form into 4 small, flat patties.
3. Place patties on hot, preheated oven sheet in *preheated* oven (hot oven sheet will sear meat so juices won't be lost). Brown patties 3–4 minutes on each side. Serve hot.
Serves 2.

Good with chutney, and Rice Salad.

VENETIAN LIVER

We spent a week in Venice—Easter week, in the early spring. Venice had a somber color because of dark skies and much rain, yet the golden light was still there. The Piazza San Marco was filled with black umbrellas as we looked down from high up in the cathedral. Later we went to lunch in a popular Venetian restaurant filled with jolly parties of families and friends, everyone having a good time.

4 paper-thin slices calf's liver
4 thin slices prosciutto or *pancetta* (Italian bacon)
1 tablespoon unsalted butter
1 garlic clove, peeled and halved
3 tablespoons dry white vermouth
Freshly ground black pepper

1. Trim any membrane from liver; slice prosciutto into thin strips.
2. Melt butter in a sauté pan or skillet and add garlic, stirring for 1 minute.
3. When butter is foaming, add prosciutto and liver, cooking liver 1 minute on each side.
4. Stir in vermouth, scraping up cooked bits on bottom of pan, and cook 1 minute.
5. Remove garlic with your spoon; season sauce to taste. Take skillet to table; serve liver with sauce from pan.
Serves 2.

This dish is good with Semolina.

CALF'S LIVER WITH RED WINE

4 paper-thin slices calf's liver
1 tablespoon unsalted butter
1 garlic clove, peeled and halved
3 tablespoons red wine vinegar
1/4 cup dry red wine
4 parsley sprigs, chopped (no stems)
Sea salt
Freshly ground black pepper

1. Trim any membrane from liver.
2. Warm butter in a sauté pan or skillet; add garlic and cook over low heat until golden, about 1 minute; remove garlic with spoon.
3. Lay liver in pan and sauté briefly over medium heat, about 1 minute on each side.
4. Pour vinegar into pan, stirring; add wine, cooking sauce 2 minutes; season to taste.
5. Sprinkle parsley over liver and serve with sauce from pan.
Serves 2.

VEAL SCALLOPS WITH ORANGE JUICE

If you buy a whole fillet of veal, about 2 pounds, you can freeze it; you can cut thin scallops whenever you wish, and you will save money.

6 veal scallops
2 tablespoons unsalted butter
1/2 cup fresh orange juice (about
 1 orange)
1/2 cup heavy cream
Sea salt
Freshly ground white pepper

1. Trim veal scallops if needed.
2. Heat butter to foaming in a sauté pan or skillet; add veal and cook until brown, about 1 minute on each side.
3. Add orange juice to pan, stirring; add cream and simmer about 3 minutes; sauce will thicken.
4. Season to taste.
Serves 2.

This is delicious with a butter lettuce salad.

VEAL WITH ZUCCHINI

The Italians treat chicken and veal in the same fashion: Thin, thin slices are sautéed in butter and garnished with lemon.

1/4 cup grated Parmesan cheese
6 very thin veal scallops, cut from fillet
2 tablespoons unsalted butter
2 unpeeled zucchini
1/2 cup chicken broth
Freshly ground black pepper
1 lemon, cut into quarters

1. Put cheese on a piece of waxed paper and roll scallops in cheese, coating both sides well.
2. Heat butter until foaming in a sauté pan or skillet, and add scallops.
3. Cook scallops about 1 minute on each side, turning when brown, and remove to a warm plate.
4. Cut thin slices of zucchini into pan; pour in broth, stirring with a spoon to scrape up all cooked bits in pan, and cook about 5 minutes over medium heat.
5. Add veal to pan and cook 1 minute; season to taste with pepper.
6. Serve veal and zucchini with sauce from pan; garnish with lemon quarters. Serves 2.

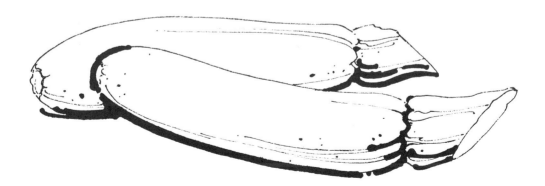

VEAL AU GRATIN

From the Grand Hotel in Florence.

Preheat broiler at full broil
1 tablespoon unsalted butter
4 thin veal scallops
4 slices prosciutto
1/4 cup chicken broth
1/2 cup heavy cream
1/4 cup grated Parmesan cheese
1/2 cup grated mozzarella cheese
Freshly ground black pepper

1. Heat butter to foaming in a sauté pan or skillet over medium heat; add veal and brown about 1 minute on each side.
2. Slice prosciutto into thin strips with a chef's knife and add to pan.
3. Add broth and cook prosciutto with veal about 1 minute; remove pan from heat and put aside.
4. Combine cream and cheese in a bowl; spread mixture over veal in pan.
5. Place pan under *preheated* broiler until sauce is brown and bubbling, about 1–2 minutes. Season with black pepper to taste. Take pan to table to serve while bubbling.
Serves 2.

GROUND VEAL MARSALA

1/2 pound coarsely ground veal, from
   the leg
1 shallot, peeled
3 parsley sprigs (no stems)
1 egg
1 teaspoon dried sage or tarragon
2 tablespoons flour
2 tablespoons unsalted butter
2 tablespoons dry Marsala
2 tablespoons sour cream
Freshly ground black pepper

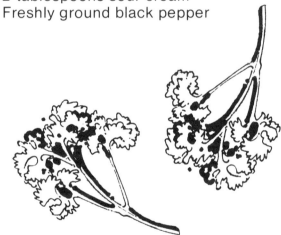

1. Put veal in a blender with shallot, parsley, egg, and sage; blend quickly to combine without making texture too fine.
2. Remove meat from blender and place on a piece of waxed paper with flour. Form veal into 4 small, flat cakes and dust lightly with flour on both sides.
3. Heat butter until foaming in a sauté pan or skillet (be careful not to burn butter); add veal, lower heat, and cook until dark golden brown, about 4 minutes on each side.
4. Pour Marsala into pan, stir, and add sour cream; season to taste with pepper.
5. Cover pan and cook slowly 5–6 minutes. Serve veal with sauce from pan.
Serves 2.

BROILED ITALIAN SAUSAGE

On a walk through the streets of Bologna, we saw fabulous displays of the famous Parma ham (prosciutto), salamis, cheeses, and the famous sausages of *la cucina italiana*. We visited the large food market just off Bologna's central square. Seen from inside it is a vast building, the walls lined with tiny food shops, each with a specialty to offer. Some of the sausage making goes on right before your eyes in an open kitchen area; we ate our fill of sausage while in town.

Preheat broiler at full broil
3 tablespoons dried oregano
6 Italian sausages
1/4 cup white wine

1. Place oregano on a piece of waxed paper and roll each sausage in oregano, covering all sides.
2. Lay sausages on an oven sheet and put under *preheated* broiler.
3. Turn sausages as they brown; after 5 minutes, baste with 1–2 tablespoons wine.
4. Continue to broil and baste until sausages are done, about 5 minutes. Serves 2.

PORK CHOPS

Two 1-inch-thick pork chops
1/2 tablespoon safflower oil
1 garlic clove, peeled
1 slice fresh bread
1 teaspoon dried oregano
4 parsley sprigs (no stems)
Freshly ground black pepper
2 tablespoons red wine vinegar
1/4 cup broth or water

1. Trim pork chops, cutting away all fat with a sharp knife.
2. Heat oil in a sauté pan or skillet and add chops. Cook chops over medium heat, 3–4 minutes on each side, turning as they brown.
3. Put garlic, bread, oregano, and parsley into a blender and purée.
4. Stir bread crumb mixture into pan and cook for 2 minutes with chops over low heat. Season with pepper to taste.
5. Pour vinegar and broth into pan and stir to blend ingredients in pan together; cook 5 minutes over medium heat.
Serve chops with sauce.
Serves 2.

I like this dish with Red Cabbage and Apples.

HAM AND CHICKEN LIVERS

The hills of Florence, in spring and fall, are soft shades of green. They are wooded and terraced with olive groves and sloping vineyards. We liked driving to the small restaurants in the hills for long, relaxed meals; the meat and birds were roasted on thin wooden skewers with bay leaves.

4 thin slices boiled ham
2 tablespoons unsalted butter
5–6 fresh sage leaves, or 1/2 teaspoon
    dried sage
1/2 cup (1/4 pound) chicken livers
1/2 cup white wine
1 cup (1 small bunch) stemmed seedless
    white grapes
Freshly ground white pepper

1. Slice ham into thin strips.
2. Melt butter in a sauté pan or skillet, add sage, and cook 1 minute. Stir in ham.
3. Add livers to pan, stirring with butter, sage, and ham, and cook for 3 minutes over medium heat, turning livers as they tan; do not overcook or livers will toughen.
4. Stir in wine and grapes (reserving 5–6 grapes for a garnish); stir bottom of pan with spoon, season with pepper to taste and cook 2 minutes.
Serves 2.

Serve with thin toast and garnish with grapes.

ENDIVE WITH HAM

6 thin slices boiled ham or prosciutto
1 head endive
2 tablespoons unsalted butter
3 tablespoons grated Gruyère cheese
Freshly ground black pepper
3 tablespoons sour cream

1. Wrap each slice of ham around 3 leaves of endive and secure with a toothpick.
2. Melt butter in a sauté pan or skillet and add bundles of ham and endive.
3. Cover pan and cook slowly 5–6 minutes; turn ham to brown both sides.
4. Remove lid, sprinkle cheese over ham, and season to taste.
5. Stir sour cream into pan with a tablespoon, catching all of the cooked bits on the bottom of the pan as you stir. Cook 3 minutes. Take pan to table to serve hot with sauce from pan.
Serves 2.

ROQUEFORT CHEESE SAUCE FOR MEAT

1 tender inner celery stalk
1/4 pound Roquefort cheese
1 cup heavy cream
1 garlic clove, peeled
1 tablespoon red wine vinegar
1 small shallot, peeled
Paprika

1. Break celery to remove strings. Put celery, cheese, and cream into a blender and purée. Add garlic, vinegar, and shallot and blend.
2. Pour into a bowl and season with paprika to taste.
Makes 1-1/2 cups.

SALADS should be carefully prepared, composed, and artfully arranged. There is beauty in the simplicity of hearts of butter lettuce tossed with oil and lemon juice, and served in a glass bowl with grated lemon rind sprinkled over the top.

A French country restaurant in Beaune served us a variety of little salads that formed an appetizing array in white-lined brown dishes. Each salad was differently dressed and sparingly seasoned, every leaf and vegetable firm and fresh, the colors skillfully blended: the greens of cucumbers, beans and peas; red tomatoes, radishes, and kidney beans; orange carrots; and pale grated celery root mixed with yellow mayonnaise. Consider how your salad will look when it is placed on the table. Use care in choosing and combining your ingredients, with some thought for taste and texture; don't just use a jumble of leftovers or tired lettuce leaves.

Wash your lettuce leaves carefully, leaf by leaf, under a thin stream of cool tap water (never soak lettuce leaves); drain in a colander. Wrap leaves in paper towels to absorb the moisture, . and refrigerate. When dressing your salad, turn the leaves over and over gently so that every leaf is coated with a thin film of oil, then serve at once. Put aside tough outer leaves of lettuce (sometimes I like to use only the tender, small inner leaves) but don't discard; chop and cook in broth with a bit of butter for your vegetable of the day.

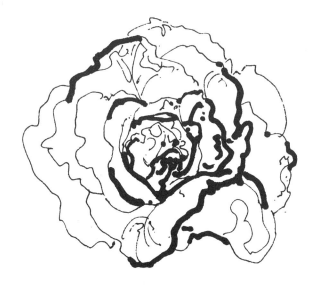

APPLE-CELERY SALAD

Eat your vegetables raw whenever possible (nutritionists increasingly emphasize the value of raw vegetables, fruits, and herbs). Try a salad with sliced or grated raw vegetables instead of cooking vegetables at the end of the day when you are tired.

1/2 cup plain yogurt
1/4 cup cottage cheese
1 lemon
1 unpeeled red apple, quartered
3 inner celery stalks
Heart of romaine lettuce
Freshly ground black pepper

1. In a salad bowl blend yogurt and cottage cheese, squeeze in juice of lemon, and stir.
2. Remove apple core and seeds with a knife and cut apple into thin slices into salad bowl.
3. Chop celery with a chef's knife and add to salad bowl with leaves of lettuce; season with pepper to taste.
4. Toss ingredients together gently to mix well with dressing.
Serves 2.

COLESLAW

1 cup mayonnaise
1–2 lemons
Paprika
1/2 small white cabbage (about 2 cups chopped)
2 carrots
1/4 cup chopped almonds

1. Put mayonnaise in a salad bowl and squeeze in juice of 1–2 lemons; stir and season to taste with paprika (dressing should be thin).
2. With a chef's knife chop cabbage coarsely and toss with dressing in bowl.
3. Grate carrots into salad bowl, add almonds, and mix all together well.
Serves 2.

CUCUMBER SALAD

Very good with broiled chicken or squab.

1/2 cup plain yogurt*
1 lemon
Few drops of Tabasco sauce
Sea salt
Paprika
1 unpeeled long, thin, English cucumber
6 parsley sprigs, chopped (no stems)

1. Place yogurt in a bowl and squeeze in juice of lemon. Stir in Tabasco, sea salt, and paprika to taste.
2. Cut cucumbers into very thin slices into bowl and stir to mix well with yogurt sauce; add parsley and serve.
Serves 2.

*I prefer Yoplait plain yogurt for cooking. Yogurt can be doubled in amount: Empty a 6-ounce container of yogurt into a bowl with 6 ounces of water and leave overnight; you will have twice as much yogurt.

GREEN BEANS, WHITE BEANS, AND RADISHES

2 cups water
1/2 pound fresh green beans, or one
  9-ounce package frozen green beans
2/3 cup safflower oil
2 lemons
1/2 cup canned white kidney beans
  (cannellini), drained
4 radishes
Freshly ground black pepper
Sea salt

1. Bring water to boil in a saucepan.
2. Snap ends off green beans, if fresh, and break in half into boiling water; cook 3 minutes (if using frozen green beans, cook in boiling water 2 minutes; no need to defrost).
3. Pour oil into a salad bowl and squeeze in lemon juice; mix in white beans. Drain green beans in a sieve and add to salad bowl, stirring so beans will absorb dressing while they are hot.
4. Slice radishes into salad bowl; season to taste. Toss carefully to mix well. Serves 2.

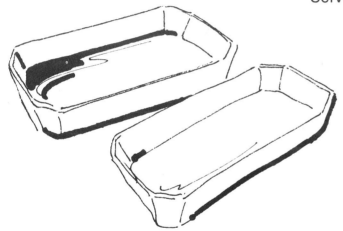

MUSHROOM SALAD

1/2 cup heavy cream or plain yogurt
1 lemon
Paprika
10–12 small unpeeled mushrooms
2 tablespoons chopped walnuts
1 cup watercress leaves (no stems)

1. Pour cream into a salad bowl, squeeze in juice of lemon, and, stirring, season to taste with paprika.
2. Wash mushrooms carefully under running water and pat dry with a paper towel. Slice mushrooms very thin into bowl and stir with dressing.
3. Add walnuts and watercress and toss to mix all together.
Serves 2.

NEW-POTATO SALAD

8 small unpeeled new potatoes (as
  small as possible)
1/2 cup sour cream
1 teaspoon horseradish
2 teaspoons Dijon mustard
1–2 lemons
4 thin slices boiled ham
Freshly ground black pepper
1 cup watercress leaves (no stems)

1. Wash potatoes and, if they are larger
than marbles, slice them into a saucepan.
2. Cover potatoes with water, bring to
boil, reduce heat, and simmer about 8
minutes.
3. In a salad bowl mix sour cream,
horseradish, and mustard, and squeeze
in juice of 1–2 lemons to make a thin
dressing.
4. With a sharp knife cut ham into long,
thin slices; place ham in salad bowl and
toss with dressing.
5. Drain potatoes into a sieve, put into
bowl with ham, season to taste with
pepper, add watercress leaves, and
carefully mix salad.
Serves 2.

RAW FENNEL SALAD

Try to make salads with raw vegetables
as often as you can, because raw
vegetables provide concentrated forms
of essential vitamins and minerals. Lemon
juice is best with this salad, as it does
not overpower the subtle flavor of the
fennel.

1/4 cup safflower oil
1 lemon
5 fennel stalks or celery stalks
1/2 cup grated Gruyère cheese
Freshly ground black pepper

1. Pour oil into a salad bowl and
squeeze in juice of lemon.
2. Cut fennel in thin slices into bowl,
add cheese, and toss with dressing.
Season to taste with pepper.
Serves 2.

TOMATO-MOZZARELLA SALAD

This is an Italian summer salad, made when tomatoes are ripe and fresh basil is in season; it is important to serve this at room temperature.

2 unpeeled ripe tomatoes
4 thin slices mozzarella cheese
1/4 cup safflower oil
1 tablespoon red wine vinegar
7–8 fresh basil leaves
Coarsely ground black pepper

1. Slice tomatoes onto a plate.
2. Lay tomato slices and cheese in alternating overlapping slices.
3. In a small bowl mix oil and vinegar; pour over tomato and cheese slices.
4. With a chef's knife coarsely chop basil and sprinkle over tomatoes and cheese; season to taste with pepper.
Serves 2.

SPINACH SALAD

A salad of raw or cooked vegetables can provide many of your nutritional needs for the day; the darker the green of the vegetable, the more nutrients there are, as in the leaves of this spinach salad.

4 slices bacon or *pancetta,* Italian bacon
1/4 cup safflower oil
1 lemon
1 cup young inner leaves of spinach
  (no stems)
Freshly ground black pepper

1. Put bacon in sauté pan or skillet and cook slowly until crisp; drain on a paper towel.
2. Pour oil into a salad bowl and squeeze in juice of lemon.
3. Place small spinach leaves in salad bowl and toss with dressing; crumble bacon into bowl and season with pepper to taste; toss again carefully to mix.
Serves 2.

COUSCOUS SALAD

Couscous, a traditional Moroccan wheat dish, cooks quickly and can be used in an emergency; keep a package on the shelf.

2 cups chicken or beef broth
1 cup couscous
3 inner, tender celery stalks
4 parsley sprigs (no stems)
1/2 cup safflower oil
2 tablespoons red wine vinegar
Sea salt
Freshly ground black pepper

1. Bring broth to boiling in a saucepan.
2. Measure couscous into a bowl and pour boiling broth over; let stand 5 minutes.
3. Chop celery and parsley together with a chef's knife and put into bowl with couscous.
4. Stir oil and vinegar into bowl with couscous; season to taste and blend all together well.
Serves 2.

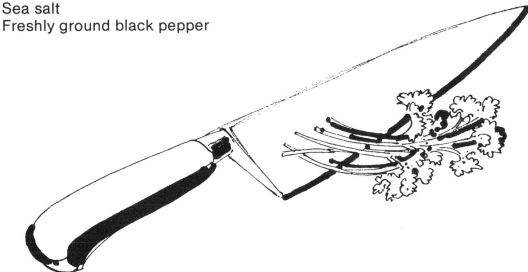

COLD BEEF SALAD

This can be a complete meal when served with warm bread.

1/2 cup heavy cream
1–2 lemons
2 teaspoons Dijon mustard
Coarsely ground black pepper
4 thin slices cooked rare roast beef
  (or steak)
1/2 cup coarsely grated Gruyère cheese
1/2 head romaine lettuce (cut
  lengthwise)

1. Pour cream into a salad bowl and squeeze in juice of 1 lemon; stir in mustard and season to taste with pepper. (Dressing should be thin; if necessary, add more lemon juice).
2. With a sharp knife cut beef into long, thin strips and add to bowl with cheese; toss with dressing to mix well.
3. With chef's knife cut lettuce in half crosswise and put into bowl; toss carefully to combine ingredients.
Serves 2.

RICE SALAD

A salad can be a complete meal when made of a combination of rice with vegetables, shellfish, chicken, or ham. There should not be too much rice in proportion to other ingredients. The rice must be mixed with dressing while hot to absorb flavor, and there should always be one crisp and one colorful element in a rice salad: grated raw vegetables, cucumbers, sweet red peppers, red radishes.

2 cups water
1 cup unwashed Italian Arborio rice
4 tablespoons safflower oil
2 tablespoons red wine vinegar
Sea salt
Freshly ground black pepper
3 inner, tender celery stalks
4 parsley sprigs (no stems)
2 unpeeled small zucchini
2 unpeeled ripe tomatoes
8 black olives

1. Pour water into a saucepan; bring water to boil and add rice. Lower heat to simmer and cook 10 minutes. Water will be absorbed.
2. Put oil into a salad bowl, add vinegar, and season to taste.
3. Break celery to remove strings. With a chef's knife chop celery and parsley and add to salad bowl.
3. Grate zucchini into salad bowl.
4. Add hot, cooked rice to salad bowl and mix well with dressing and vegetables.
5. Slice tomatoes onto plates and put a spoonful of rice on each tomato slice. Garnish with black olives.
Serves 2.

Serve with cheese and warm crusty bread.

CHICKEN SALAD

Bean sprouts make a crisp salad, and no peeling or chopping is needed; a quick rinse and they are ready to toss. Alfalfa sprouts are loaded with Vitamin B; they are low in calories and high in nutrition.

1 whole chicken breast, halved, boned, and skinned
1/2 cup mayonnaise
1 tablespoon soy sauce
1 teaspoon Dijon mustard
1 lemon
4 celery stalks
1/2 cup bean sprouts or alfalfa sprouts
6 butter lettuce leaves

1. Cut chicken breasts in half lengthwise to make 4 pieces. Place chicken in a saucepan and cover with water; bring to boil, reduce heat, and simmer over medium-high heat 10 minutes.
2. While chicken is simmering make dressing: In a salad bowl blend together mayonnaise, soy sauce, and mustard; squeeze in juice of lemon and stir.
3. Break celery to remove strings; with a chef's knife chop celery into small pieces.
4. Drain chicken in a sieve over a bowl (freeze broth to use another time). Cut chicken into small pieces; mix with dressing in bowl.
5. Add chopped celery, sprouts, and lettuce leaves to bowl and toss well with chicken and dressing.
Serves 2.

CRAB SALAD WITH ORANGES

In Taormina, we had lunch in an English garden. The meal was a great pleasure, as we were surrounded by vines and pomegranates, orange trees, lemon trees, and roses. This salad was made with the blood-red oranges of Sicily.

1/2 pound cooked crabmeat, or one
  6 ounce can crabmeat
1 cup mayonnaise
2–3 oranges
3 tablespoons capers, drained
Sea salt
Freshly ground black pepper
Hearts of butter lettuce
Extra capers for garnish

1. Put crabmeat in a bowl and flake with a fork.
2. Place mayonnaise in a bowl and squeeze juice of 1 orange into mayonnaise and mix; add more orange juice, if necessary, to thin mayonnaise to consistency of heavy cream.
3. Mix mayonnaise with crabmeat, add capers, and season to taste.
4. With a sharp knife, slice 1 orange very thin, leaving on peel for color.
5. Toss lettuce, crabmeat, and orange slices together in a bowl; garnish with a few capers sprinkled over the top.
Serves 2.

SOME IDEAS
FOR QUICKLY MADE SALADS

- Mix sour cream, Dijon mustard, and fresh lemon juice; add a handful of shrimp or prawns and romaine lettuce leaves.
- Slice an English cucumber into rounds; mix with plain yogurt, fresh lemon juice, and paprika.
- Mix avocado slices and crabmeat with mayonnaise made with a tomato, adding Worcestershire sauce and Tabasco sauce.
- Fill a papaya half with cut-up apples and oranges mixed with plain yogurt, orange juice, and chopped almonds.
- Make a cold pasta salad; mix with Mayonnaise au Pistou and garnish with black olives.
- Slice firm pears and toss with small butter lettuce leaves and Yogurt-Blue Cheese Dressing.
- Peel and cut 1 orange into thin slices; toss with curly endive, anchovies, and hot vinaigrette dressing; season to taste with black pepper.

QUICKLY MADE SALAD DRESSINGS

These basic dressings offer endless possibilities as inspirations for quickly made salads.

BASIC VINAIGRETTE

1 tablespoon red wine vinegar or fresh
   lemon juice
Sea salt
Freshly ground black pepper
1 teaspoon Dijon mustard (optional)
1 garlic clove, peeled (optional)
6 tablespoons good olive oil or
   safflower oil

1. Put vinegar in a small bowl and stir in seasoning.
2. Pour in olive oil and mix.
Makes 1/2 cup.

CREAM DRESSING

1/2 cup heavy cream
1 teaspoon Dijon mustard
1 lemon
Sea salt
Freshly ground black pepper

1. Pour cream into a small bowl. Stir in mustard and squeeze in juice of lemon.
2. Stir well and season to taste.
Makes 1/2 cup.

LOW-CAL DRESSING

1 unpeeled ripe tomato
1/2 cup plain yogurt
1 teaspoon Worcestershire sauce
Freshly ground black pepper

1. Cut tomato into a blender; add yogurt and Worcestershire sauce and blend.
2. Season with pepper to taste.
Makes 1 cup.

YOGURT-BLUE CHEESE DRESSING

1/2 cup plain yogurt
1/4 cup blue cheese
1 shallot, peeled
1 lemon

1. Combine yogurt and blue cheese in a blender.
2. Add shallot, squeeze in juice of lemon, and blend together.
Makes 1 cup.

WATERCRESS DRESSING

A brilliant green dressing.

3/4 cup olive oil
1 cup watercress leaves (no stems)
1 shallot, peeled
2 lemons
Paprika
Coarsely ground black pepper

1. Combine oil, watercress, and shallot in a blender; squeeze in juice of lemons and blend.
2. Pour dressing into a bowl and season to taste.
Makes 1 cup.

FRESH–FRUIT SALAD DRESSING

1 cup plain yogurt
1/4 cup honey
1–2 oranges
Coarsely ground black pepper

1. Place yogurt and honey in a small bowl.
2. Squeeze juice of 1–2 oranges into bowl, stirring; dressing should be the consistency of thin cream.
3. Season with pepper to taste.
Makes 3/4 cup.

MAYONNAISE

Mayonnaise is quickly made. There are many variations on the basic theme of mayonnaise. I have timed myself and can make this mayonnaise in two minutes in my blender; it takes less time and less money than going to the supermarket to buy bottled mayonnaise.

1 egg
1/2 cup safflower oil (lighter than olive
  oil)
1 lemon, or 1 tablespoon red wine
  vinegar
Sea salt
Freshly ground black pepper

1. Break egg into a blender and turn blender on and off quickly to mix egg.
2. Add oil in a thin stream; don't over-pour, or oil will drown egg.
3. As mixture thickens, squeeze in juice of lemon.
4. Pour into a bowl and season to taste. Makes 1 cup.

Refrigerated mayonnaise will keep 3–4 days.

Variations To use as a dressing for vegetables, thin mayonnaise to the consistency of thin cream with a little broth or water that vegetables have been cooked in. Or flavor mayonnaise with 2 teaspoons green peppercorns in vinegar.

MUSTARD MAYONNAISE

1 cup mayonnaise
1 tablespoon Dijon mustard
Sea salt
Freshly ground black pepper

1. Blend mayonnaise and mustard together and season to taste.
Makes 1 cup.

Variation In place of Dijon mustard, use another imported mustard. I like to collect a variety of imported mustards, including some flavored with herbs such as tarragon and chives. Keep on the refrigerator shelf.

ANCHOVY MAYONNAISE

Good with poached fish and raw vegetables.

1 cup mayonnaise
2 teaspoons anchovy paste, or
   3 anchovies

1. Blend mayonnaise and anchovy paste together in a blender.
Makes 1 cup.

TOMATO MAYONNAISE

Good with shellfish, vegetables, and poached fish.

1 unpeeled ripe tomato
1 cup mayonnaise
1 lemon
Sea salt
Freshly ground black pepper

1. Cut tomato into a blender, add mayonnaise, squeeze in juice of lemon, and purée.
2. Pour into a bowl and season to taste.
Makes 3/4 cup.

GREEN MAYONNAISE

1 cup mayonnaise
1/4 cup watercress leaves (no stems)
6 parsley sprigs (no stems)
2 tablespoons any fresh herbs such as
  tarragon or oregano (optional)
Freshly ground black pepper

1. Blend mayonnaise, watercress, parsley, and herbs together in a blender.
2. Season with pepper to taste.
Makes 1 cup.

CURRY MAYONNAISE

Good with vegetables and fish.

1 cup mayonnaise
3 teaspoons curry powder
Freshly ground black pepper

1. Blend mayonnaise and curry powder together and season with pepper to taste.
Makes 1 cup.

Variation To make a lighter mayonnaise, add 1/2 cup plain yogurt.

MAYONNAISE AU PISTOU

This is like mayonnaise because of the egg, but is made without oil. This sauce is good with poached fish, boiled white beans, and quickly cooked green beans; it is a good dip for raw vegetables such as zucchini and celery.

1 egg
1 garlic clove, peeled
1 unpeeled ripe tomato
9 fresh basil leaves
One 3-ounce package cream cheese
2 tablespoons heavy cream
Sea salt
Coarsely ground black pepper

1. Mix egg in blender with garlic. Cut tomato into blender; add basil, cream cheese, and cream; purée.
2. Pour purée into a small bowl and season to taste.
Makes 1 cup.

DESSERTS can be chosen from a wide variety of flavors. As a meal seems unfinished without an ending, choose a light, frothy dish with a berry sauce; or an ice, tart with lemon or orange juice; a sensuous mousse of moist, rich chocolate; a nutty brown-sugar cookie; a highly seaoned cheese; or a glass of sweet dessert wine to end your meal.

Much of the pleasure of a dessert is visual: Small details such as a glass bowl, a sprig of mint, grated orange rind, or grated chocolate will enhance your dessert.

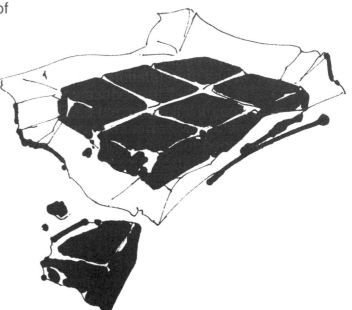

RICH, RICH CHOCOLATE DESSERT

This combination of cake and mousse needs no frosting; it melts in your mouth.

Preheat oven to 450°F
2 eggs, at room temperature
6 tablespoons unsalted butter
6 ounces dark mildly sweet chocolate bar (Hershey's 8-ounce bar)
2 tablespoons brown sugar
2 tablespoons granulated sugar
3 tablespoons flour

1. Separate whites and yolks of eggs into 2 bowls.
2. Place butter in a small bowl, and break chocolate into pieces into bowl. To melt chocolate and butter, put bowl in a sauté pan or skillet filled with simmering water.
3. While chocolate is melting, add sugar to bowl, stirring; when butter, sugar, and chocolate are combined, add flour; remove from heat.
4. With a whisk or an egg beater, beat egg whites until they stand in soft peaks; immediately, with same beater, beat egg yolks and stir into chocolate mixture.
5. Quickly fold in egg whites and spoon into a buttered medium-sized (6–7 inches) sauté pan or skillet.
6. Place pan in *preheated* oven to bake 10–12 minutes. The outer edge of this dessert should be like cake, the inner part like a melted chocolate bar.
Serves 2.

WINTER PLUMS

This is a winter dessert.

1/2 cup sour cream
1/2 cup plain yogurt
1/4 cup firmly packed brown sugar
6 canned plums, drained

1. In a bowl mix sour cream, yogurt, and brown sugar.
2. Add plums to bowl and stir together. Serves 2.

Serve with macaroons.

APPLES WITH APRICOT JAM

Cooked fruit makes a delightful dessert; fresh fruit, baked or poached, is as easy as can be. (Don't use aluminum pans to cook fruits.)

4 unpeeled apples
1/2 cup water
2 tablespoons honey
1/3 cup apricot jam

1. Quarter apples, remove core, and slice apples into a saucepan.
2. Add water and honey to pan; cover pan and cook over medium heat 10 minutes.
3. Stir in apricot jam, whipping well. Serves 2.

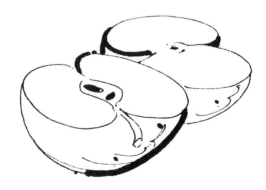

ROMAN FIGS WITH CREAM

I had this heavenly dish in Rome.

1 cup heavy cream
1/4 cup powdered sugar
1 teaspoon vanilla extract
5–6 fresh black figs or other fresh
    fruit such as peaches, strawberries,
    or raspberries

1. Pour cream into a bowl and beat
with a whisk or an egg beater, adding
sugar and vanilla while beating, until
cream is softly peaked but not stiff.
2. Peel figs and slice them into bowl
with whipped cream; fold in carefully.
Refrigerate until ready to serve.
Serves 2.

This luscious dessert is pretty served in
a glass bowl. It freezes well, if you have
any left over or want to make it in
advance.

COOKED BANANAS

1 tablespoon unsalted butter
2 ripe bananas, peeled
1 orange
1 tablespoon honey or brown sugar
2 tablespoons rum or brandy

1. Melt butter in a sauté pan or skillet
over medium heat; add bananas to pan.
2. Grate rind of orange into pan; squeeze
in juice of orange and add honey. Cover
pan and cook slowly 10 minutes, basting
bananas 1–2 times with sauce in pan.
3. Heat rum or brandy in a small pan,
light with a match, and pour over
bananas; serve.
Serves 2.

POACHED PEARS

3 winter pears
1/2 cup water
1/4 cup sugar or honey
1/2 lemon

1. Pour water and sugar into a small saucepan and boil over high heat 3 minutes.
2. Quarter and core pears (do not peel) and slice into pan. Squeeze juice of 1/2 lemon over pears.
3. Cover pan and simmer pears over medium heat 6–7 minutes. Serve pears at room temperature with syrup from pan.

Variation Serve with Chocolate Sauce and Praline, or with Hot Cherry Sauce.

CREAM CHEESE DESSERT

1/2 cup sour cream
One 3-ounce package cream cheese, or
   1/4 pound fresh cream cheese
2 tablespoons brandy

1. Mix sour cream and cheese together with a whisk or in a blender, adding brandy.
2. Put into a small bowl.
Serves 2.

Serve with currant jelly and crackers, or a small can of sliced pineapple.

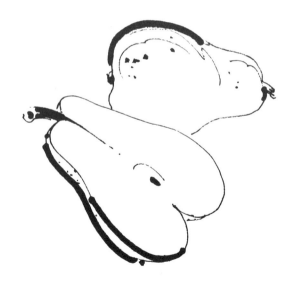

VANILLA SOUFFLE

A soufflé in a wide, shallow dish cooks more quickly than in a soufflé dish; use your sauté pan or skillet for baking soufflés.

Preheat oven to 475°F
3 eggs, at room temperature
2 tablespoons unsalted butter
2 tablespoons flour
1 cup warm milk
1/2 cup sugar
1/4 cup Grand Marnier (alcohol helps soufflé to rise)

1. Separate whites and yolks of eggs into 2 bowls.
2. Melt butter in a sauté pan or skillet, stir in flour, and cook 1 minute.
3. Add warm milk, whisking until smooth; remove from heat to cool.
4. With a whisk or an egg beater, beat egg whites until they form soft peaks (don't overbeat, or they will be dry).
5. Beat yolks quickly (with same beater), adding sugar and Grand Marnier.
6. Stir sauce into yolks and lightly fold mixture into egg whites.
7. Pour into a sauté pan or skillet, and put into *preheated hot* oven. Soufflé will take 10 minutes to bake and rise; it will be crusty outside, creamy in center (use center as a sauce).
Serves 2.

Also good with Apricot Sauce or Peach Sauce. Or purée one 10-ounce package frozen strawberries in a blender; serve frozen purée with hot soufflé.

INSTANT SHERBET

One 10-ounce package frozen
   sweetened strawberries or raspberries
1 lemon
2 tablespoons crème de cassis
1 lemon, quartered, for garnish

1. Cut frozen package into quarters
with a serrated knife; remove paper and
place frozen chunks of strawberries
into a blender.
2. Blend berries until smooth, about 1
minute. Squeeze juice of lemon into
blender and add cassis; blend briefly.
3. Serve immediately, garnished with
lemon, or freeze until ready to serve.
Serves 2.

Variation Pour puréed frozen raspberries over fresh strawberries and sprinkle
with pistachio nuts.

ROQUEFORT OR GORGONZOLA CHEESE DESSERT

1/2 pound Roquefort or Gorgonzola
   cheese
1/4 cup heavy cream
1 teaspoon Worcestershire sauce
2 tablespoons brandy
1/2 cup pistachio nuts (reserve a few
   to sprinkle over top)

1. Put half the cheese in a blender with
cream and mix.
2. Add Worcestershire sauce, remaining
cheese, brandy, and nuts and blend
well together.
3. Spoon into a bowl; decorate top with
pistachio nuts.
Serves 2.

This keeps very well in the refrigerator.

CREAM WITH COFFEE
AND CHOCOLATE

This dessert comes from the elegant Caffè Greco in Rome, where colorful figures from all over the world meet to sit at tables to look, to gossip, and to be seen.

1/2 cup heavy cream
1 tablespoon powdered instant coffee
2 tablespoons cocoa (preferably Dutch cocoa)
4 tablespoons superfine sugar
2 tablespoons rum

1. Pour cream into a bowl and beat with a whisk or an egg beater, adding coffee, cocoa, and sugar while beating, until cream is softly peaked but not stiff.
2. With a tablespoon stir in rum.
3. Refrigerate until ready to serve. Serves 2.

The Italians like *semifreddo* desserts—cold, not frozen—because the flavor is more apparent.

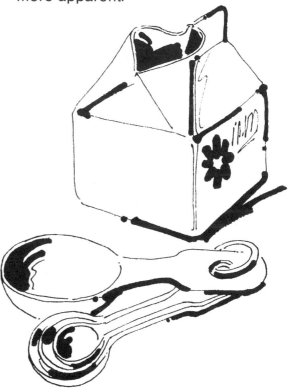

CAFE LIEGEOIS

The joy, the pleasure of a table at Angelina's in Paris, waiting for this exquisitely sweet combination of dessert and coffee.

Have ready 2 wine glasses, each with a
  silver teaspoon to absorb the heat
1/2 cup heavy cream
2 tablespoons powdered sugar
1/2 pint (1 cup) frozen vanilla ice cream
2 cups strong hot instant coffee
6 hard coffee candies, coarsely ground
  in blender

1. Pour cream into a bowl and beat with a whisk or an egg beater until softly peaked; add sugar as you beat.
2. Put 2 tablespoons of ice cream into each wine glass; pour coffee into glasses.
3. Add 1 tablespoon whipped cream to each glass; sprinkle candies over tops. Serve immediately.
Serves 2.

PEACH SAUCE

2 fresh peaches, peeled and pitted
  (or about 1 cup frozen peaches)
2 tablespoons powdered sugar
3 tablespoons Grand Marnier

1. Cut peaches into a blender and purée.
2. Pour purée into a bowl and stir in sugar and Grand Marnier.
Makes 1 cup.

Serve with vanilla ice cream and sprinkle with chopped almonds.

FRESH STRAWBERRY SAUCE

A rapidly prepared sauce for soufflé or fruit or cream cheese.

8–10 strawberries, washed and stemmed
1–2 tablespoons sugar

1. Purée berries in blender with sugar to make a delicious sauce.
Serves 2.

HOT CHERRY SAUCE

This thick syrup of dark, sweet cherries makes a rich topping for cooked fruit, ice cream, or custard and can be used like jam on your toast or croissant.

One 16-ounce can pitted dark sweet
   Bing cherries in syrup
Grated rind of 1 lemon
Juice of 1/2 lemon
1 cup sugar

1. Pour cherries with syrup into a blender and purée.
2. Pour purée into an enamel or tin-lined saucepan; grate rind of lemon into pan, add sugar, and bring to boiling over high heat.
3. Squeeze juice of lemon into pan; lower heat so cherry syrup won't boil over, but keep boiling slowly for 8–10 minutes, until syrup has thickened.
4. Pour syrup into a bowl or jar; syrup will keep refrigerated for 2–3 weeks. Makes 2 cups.

APRICOT SAUCE

The blender and the food processor are magic for making sauces; canned fruit can be instantly made into a delicious sauce or a jam. Try this apricot sauce with cooked pears, apples, or vanilla soufflé; it is also good on toast.

One 8-ounce can unpeeled apricot
  halves in heavy syrup
1/4 cup sugar
1 orange

1. Place apricots with their syrup in a blender and purée.
2. Pour purée into a saucepan and bring to boil over high heat, stirring.
3. Add sugar to pan, squeeze in juice of orange, and stir well.
4. Boil purée for 7 minutes; watch pan so purée doesn't boil over or burn. Remove from heat and pour into a bowl to serve hot or cold.
Makes 1 cup.

Variation Frozen peaches or frozen sweetened strawberries can be used in place of canned apricots.

CHOCOLATE SAUCE

A rich chocolate sauce can be used to gild simple desserts; try a fresh pear with Chocolate Sauce and chopped almonds, or slices of angel food cake with Chocolate Sauce and Praline.

4 tablespoons (1/4 cup) unsalted butter
2 ounces bittersweet chocolate bar*
2 ounces milk chocolate bar*
1 teaspoon vanilla extract

1. Put butter in a small bowl; break chocolate into bowl with butter and place bowl in a saucepan of simmering water to melt.
2. As chocolate and butter melt, stir until smooth and add vanilla.
Makes 1/2 cup.

*Perugina chocolate bars are good.

Variation Grate rind of 1/2 orange into chocolate and add 1 teaspoon orange juice instead of vanilla.

PRALINE

1/2 cup granulated sugar
1/2 cup almonds

1. Place sugar in a sauté pan or skillet and stir over medium heat until sugar is melted.
2. Add almonds and stir until mixture is golden brown, about 3 minutes.
3. Allow praline to cool and harden in a buttered pan. When praline is hard, hit pan on a firm surface to crack praline.
4. Put broken pieces of praline in a blender and crush.
Makes 1/2 cup.

Keep Praline in a covered jar to use as needed as a topping for desserts.

EASY COOKIES

Preheat oven to 375°F
4 tablespoons (1/4 cup) soft unsalted butter
1/4 cup sugar
1 teaspoon vanilla extract
1/2 cup flour
1/2 cup almonds, hazelnuts, or walnuts, finely chopped
1 tablespoon powdered sugar

1. Put butter in a bowl, add sugar, and mix together with a spoon.
2. Pour vanilla into mixture. Add flour, 2 tablespoons at a time, stirring well. Add almonds; this makes a firm dough.
3. Drop from a teaspoon onto an oven sheet, forming batter into a ball with your fingers on the sheet.
4. Bake in *preheated* oven 6–7 minutes; cookies will be a light tan color.
5. Put powdered sugar in a sieve and sprinkle over cookies when baked.
Makes 2 dozen cookies.

OATMEAL BARS

This is an instantaneous dessert to make when you are craving something sweet.

Preheat oven to 400°F
1/3 cup butter
1/2 cup firmly packed brown sugar
1 cup oatmeal
1/4 cup raisins

1. Melt butter in a pan over low heat and stir in sugar, oatmeal, and raisins.
2. Put into a baking pan or skillet measuring 6–7 inches, smoothing batter into a thin layer.
3. Bake until golden in *preheated* oven, about 5–6 minutes.
4. Let sit 3–4 minutes; cut into squares. Makes 12 squares.

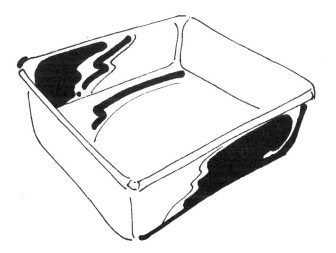

BROWN SUGAR COOKIES

This is a light, lacy, thin cookie.

Preheat oven to 350°F
1/2 cup water
1-1/2 cups firmly packed brown sugar
1/4 pound (1/2 cup) unsalted butter
1 cup flour
1 cup chopped pecans

1. Put water and 1/2 cup brown sugar in a saucepan and boil rapidly for 3 minutes to reduce and thicken syrup.
2. Remove from heat and add butter, stirring as it melts.
3. Mix in flour, remaining 1 cup brown sugar, and pecans.
4. Drop batter with a teaspoon onto a buttered baking sheet, leaving about 1 inch between cookies, as they will spread and be very thin.
5. Bake 4 minutes in *preheated* oven.
6. Allow to cool 1–2 minutes before removing to a plate.
Makes 3 dozen cookies.

If you want to bake just a few, batter will freeze well.

LITTLE CAKES

Minutes away from the noisy, narrow streets of Florence is Fiesole. We would go often to the Villa San Michele for tea: The cloistered courtyard and shady loggia are perfect places for a hot day. Looking at the green hills of Fiesole from there is like looking through fine gauze. In May the fragrant, small wild strawberries are in season for only a moment. They are soaked in orange juice, dusted with sugar, and served on these small flat cakes.

Preheat oven to 375°F
4 tablespoons (1/4 cup) soft unsalted
  butter
1/2 cup granulated sugar
1 egg
1/2 cup flour
1 tablespoon fresh orange juice

1. Place butter in a bowl with sugar and blend together.
2. Mix in egg, flour, and orange juice.
3. Lightly butter an oven sheet; with a teaspoon drop small rounds of dough 2 inches apart; cakes will spread.
4. Put oven sheet in *preheated* oven; bake 8 minutes, until cakes are lightly colored.
5. With a spatula, lift cakes onto a plate.
Makes 10 to 12 small cakes; they will keep for several days.

VERY BRIEFLY, WINES add a great deal of pleasure to a meal; a few glasses of wine will relax everyone, creating an easy atmosphere for enjoying friends, food, and conversation.

Do as you please with wine; serve what tastes good to you. It can be red, white, or rosé, and it need not be expensive. It is a matter of what suits each individual. There is no absolute rule; there are only general rules of good sense and taste, keeping in mind a few practical considerations. Since a tart, acidic flavor (sour fruits, artichokes, sauces and dressings made with vinegar) will make wine taste metallic, drink your wine before and after the salad. A sugary frozen dessert will stun the palate, making even the finest dessert wines taste thin and flavorless.

When selecting a wine glass, the tulip shape (8-ounce size) is the best choice, as it is multipurpose (with small kitchens lack of storage space is a consideration). The tulip shape is suitable for all wines, water, and mixed drinks. If you wish two shapes, the classic tulip will enhance the color and bouquet of wine, and the elegant classic champagne flute will contain the bubbles and chill of champagne. Fill your glass only two-thirds full, at most, in order to savor the bouquet of the wine (and to save the wine if the glass spills).

For small, informal dinners you may serve only one wine. This should be chosen with care to be pleasing with the appetizer, main dish, and dessert. For special occasions you may wish to serve only champagne as an apéritif and throughout the meal, but the champagne must be very dry, not sweet.

Don't overdo adding wines and liqueurs in your cooking, as too much can spoil a dish. Flaming your food with spirits has its purpose: By the time the alcohol burns away, any trace of grease or oil will disappear with the flame, but the flavor of the sauce will have become highly concentrated.

When entertaining and feeding guests, timing is all important. I like to serve one hot canapé and then go to table with an appetizer or first course to be enjoyed with wine, rather than serving too many canapés and drinks, resulting in spoiled, dulled appetites for both food and wine.

The choice of the wine to drink with your meal is a matter of taste. Dry white wines seem to work with appetizers, soups, pasta, fish, and fowl, and dry red wines seem best for meat dishes. As a general rule, with heavy food serve a heavier wine; with lighter dishes, serve a light wine. Fish with body and oiliness, and fish stews with garlic, tomatoes, and anchovies, will take a red burgundy; chicken cooked with tomatoes and black olives can take a red burgundy. Strong-flavored meats, game, cheese, and codfish will take a red bordeaux. Fresh vegetables, fish, shellfish, cold roast chicken, and grilled meats take lighter, less complicated wines such as gently chilled whites or cooled reds. A dry white wine goes well with shellfish, yet some people find pleasing the combination of beaujolais with shellfish, clams, oysters, mussels, and salmon. Sweet dessert wines and sparkling wines come at the close of the meal, with the dessert or fruit.

In summer rosé and the light-bodied reds, briefly cooled before serving, are perfect for light dishes and picnics.

Along the French Riviera, they like rosé on hot summer days. California chablis, light and dry, makes a refreshing warm-weather drink: Add ice and fill up the glass with soda. Blanc de Blancs has a lightness and delicacy, making a pleasant apéritif with a few drops of crème de cassis (black-currant liqueur) and kirsch.

Champagne suits many needs: It is served for festive occasions, it is offered as a necessary tonic in Swiss sanitariums, and it is an elegant picnic wine. The Italians serve many variations of apéritifs made with champagne: in summer, the exquisite Bellini, made with pale fresh peaches; in fall, champagne with freshly squeezed grape juice, and with fresh tangerine and orange juice as a midday apéritif.

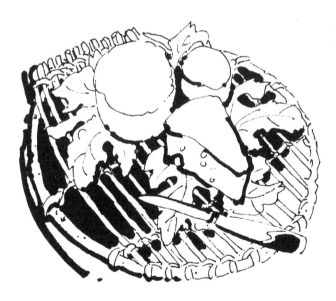

The Italian white wines—Orvieto, Soave, and Verdicchio—are pleasing to taste and can be enjoyed with most meals. The light reds, Valpolicella and Bardolino, are excellent wines; and both Chianti Classico and Brolio, grown near Florence, can be superb; all will enhance a dish of pasta. Most Italians wouldn't consider a meal without wine.

The wines of Alsace, the rieslings and sylvaners, have a fruity flavor that makes them perfect for roast duck, squab, sausage, pork, and sauerkraut. The wines of Germany, the rieslings of the Rhine and Mosel valleys, are sweeter, but a delight. Sweet wines, such as sauternes, are better served after dinner or with desserts and pastries, and can be served very cold.

Serve each wine at the temperature that brings out its best qualities:

Champagne Serve very cold; chill 2 hours in the refrigerator.

Sweet white wines, sauternes Can be served quite cold; chill 1–2 hours in the refrigerator.

Dry white wines Should be cooled, not cold; chill 40 minutes in the refrigerator, 20–30 minutes in an ice bucket. You should be able to taste the wine; freezing kills both the taste and the bouquet.

Red wines, bordeaux, burgundy Serve at room temperature; do not chill great old red wines.

Young red wines such as California burgundy jug wines can be poured into a decanter before serving to heighten the flavor of the wine.

Rosé, beaujolais Fresh light wines should be cool, not cold; chill 40–60 minutes in the refrigerator.

It has often been said that the pleasures of civilized life are conversation, food, and wine, so whatever wine you choose, enjoy it and drink it with pleasure.

PUTTING IT ALL TOGETHER, here are a few last thoughts about cooking. I think food should be arranged and planned to make you hungry, it must be fresh and appetizing, and I think it important that food suit the occasion.

Don't plan meals with lots of fussy details; feature one well-prepared dish. Always organize your menu within the reality of what you can manage without falling apart; if one dish takes time to prepare and cook, make the rest of the menu as simple as possible. When planning your meal, avoid combining dishes using the same ingredients or serving more than one dish cooked with wine. Consider the flavors, the colors, and the texture of the foods you are putting together. Combine opposites such as crisp with smooth, bland with spicy.

Garnish your serving platter with a big bunch of watercress, parsley, or tarragon; it is more effective than lots of tiny decorations. A light, imaginative touch will create a lively, cheerful atmosphere for your meals. You don't have to spend your time and money arranging flowers for a centerpiece; surprise everyone with one large red cabbage in the center of the table, or a polished purple eggplant, a head of curly, pale-green lettuce, or a bundle of breadsticks, tied with raffia, to break off and eat.

I hope my recipes have helped you to develop a more relaxed point of view about cooking. When you prepare my 15-minute meals you can have a fast and easy dinner, yet eat well with a small investment of time, energy, and money. You can serve delicious food with grace, style, and wit, with a menu and wine well suited to the occasion. That is what my book is all about.

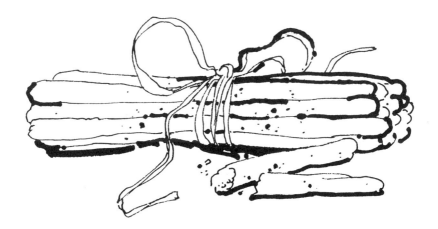

MENUS

Veal with Zucchini
Rice Salad
Oatmeal Bars

Pasta Butterflies with Gorgonzola
Fresh Spinach
Instant Sherbet

Ham and Chicken Livers
Raw Fennel Salad
Hot Cherry Sauce with ice cream

Soufflé for Two
Cheese Biscuits
Papaya fruit salad

Fish with Mustard Sauce
Green Beans
Little Cakes

Tuscan Chicken
Cucumber Salad
Roquefort or Gorgonzola Cheese Dessert
    with apples

Broiled Lamb Chops
Quickly Cooked Artichokes
Rich, Rich Chocolate Dessert

Corn Crisps
Pork Chops
Red Cabbage and Apples
Winter Plums

Crab Legs Sauté
Tomato Broth
Vanilla Soufflé

Chicken with Plum Sauce
Watercress salad
Easy Cookies

Calf's Liver with Red Wine
Peas with Lettuce
Cream Cheese Dessert with pineapple

Scallops
Mushroom Salad
Semolina
Poached Pears

Cold Pasta Salad
Broiled Italian Sausage
Chocolate Sauce with ice cream

Fish Soup
Green and Yellow Squash
Apples with Apricot Jam

Squab with Mustard-Orange Marinade
Asparagus Purée
Cooked Bananas

Baked Salmon
Rice with Chopped Vegetables
Café Liegeois

Italian Meatballs
Green Salad with Basic Vinaigrette
Strawberries with Cream

Chicken Custard in Broth
Broccoli
Cake with Praline

Baked White Fish
Nutritious New Red Potatoes
Brown Sugar Cookies

Giant Puff
Cold Beef Salad
Cream with Coffee and Chocolate

INDEX

EMALEE CHAPMAN's lifelong interest in good food was inspired by her Italian heritage. Her father, who was born in Verona, and her mother, whose family was from Lucca, set an exemplary table. Later, Ms. Chapman studied French cooking at Le Cordon Bleu and at Maxim's in Paris, and while living in Florence with her children learned the dishes of northern Italy. In 1970 she established The Cooking School in San Francisco and started conducting one-week cooking workshops in Beverly Hills and Texas. Currently she acts as a food consultant for corporations, and writes about food for a number of magazines. For several years her "Dining In" column appeared in *San Francisco* magazine and later in *The San Francisco Chronicle.* Her recipes have also been featured in *House & Garden* and *British House & Garden.*

ALICE HARTH, a San Francisco illustrator, graphic designer, and lover of good food and travel, met Emalee Chapman while attending her cooking classes. Alice Harth's design clients have included spice and herb producers, food corporations, magazines, and book publishers. She teaches a design-illustration course at City College of San Francisco. A native of California, she studied fine arts and design at the University of California at Los Angeles.

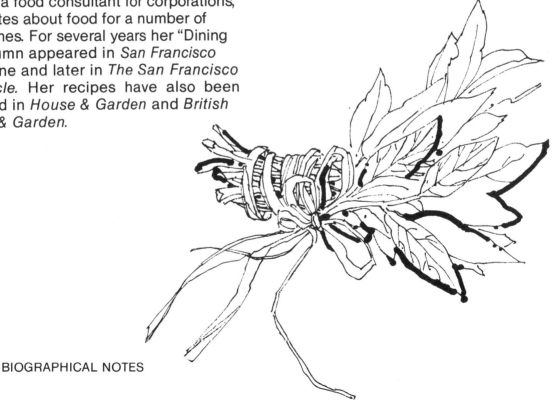